Overthrows

Cricket books by J. M. Kilburn

In Search of Cricket

The Scarborough Cricket Festival

Yorkshire: County Cricket Series

Len Hutton: A Portrait

History of Yorkshire CCC 1924–1949

Homes of Sport: Cricket with N. W. D. Yardley

Cricket Decade

100 Years of Yorkshire Cricket

A History of Yorkshire Cricket

Thanks to Cricket

J. M. KILBURN

OVERTHROWS

A Book of Cricket

STANLEY PAUL, LONDON

Stanley Paul & Co Ltd
3 Fitzroy Square, London W1

An imprint of the Hutchinson Publishing Group

London Melbourne Sydney Auckland
Wellington Johannesburg Cape Town
and agencies throughout the world

First published 1975

Photograph Credits: Patrick Eagar/Press Association/
Sheffield Newspapers Ltd/Sport & General/Syndication
International

Set in Monotype Joanna
Printed in Great Britain by The Anchor Press Ltd
and bound by Wm Brendon & Son Ltd
both of Tiptree, Essex

ISBN 0 09 122770 4

CONTENTS

Preface

Overthrows have a dubious standing in the accountancy of cricket. Scorers grant them no symbol of identity; batsmen accept them as an unearned increment to be hidden in the sum of an innings; bowlers resent them as an unjust imposition.

Overthrows are penalty for sins of omission in backing up. Yorkshiremen are supposed to enjoy them as 'summat for nowt' or to deplore them as extravagance, according to their derivation. Tail-end batsmen with a Cecil Parkin sense of humour try to provoke their accumulation, thereby adding to the gaiety and occasionally to the substance of the score.

Overthrows are outside the necessities of cricket but they do sometimes augment the enjoyment of the game. Hopefully, in that interpretation this book is titled.

J.M.K.

1. Sir Lancelot and Llewellyn

When I was seven and eight years old my heroes were Sir Lancelot of King Arthur's Court and C.B.Llewellyn of Undercliffe Cricket Club. I cannot now specify a moment and precise place of discovery for Sir Lancelot, but I remember exactly where and when Charles Bennett Llewellyn was enthroned.

My childhood Lancelot was not from Malory or Tennyson at first hand. He came to me as an unflawed version of the knight who was never matched in feat of arms and chivalrous character and his failure in the quest for the Holy Grail puzzled me for a decade. I was not prepared or required to acknowledge any fault in Sir Lancelot as I met him, in pages to which I cannot attach a title, but to whose author and publisher I am grateful beyond measure. Sir Lancelot became the knight of knights for me on first reading.

C.B.Llewellyn made the same immediate impact. I came upon him at the Park Avenue cricket ground in Bradford on the occasion of a Priestley Cup Final. He was playing a recovery innings after his side had made a bad start and from crease to one embankment seat a captivation flowed in the magic of communication recognized by poets and lovers but inexplicable yet in science.

For a season or two my cricket in the street and on the public recreation ground was played as Llewellyn; not in imitation of Llewellyn, not in the assumed name of Llewellyn, but in the alternative identity, as Sir Lancelot could become alternative identity in day-dreams over a book. On summer Saturdays I went to watch Llewellyn play, adventuring on foot or by tram-ride through the territory of the Bradford Cricket League.

Seeking Llewellyn I found a richer store. These were years of the First World War when the Bradford League drew the available first-class cricketers of the country for spectacular contest, when Barnes bowled to Woolley, Hitch to Hobbs. Watching Llewellyn, or waiting for him, gave me glimpses of greatness that no other cricket centre in the world could have offered at that particular time. Undercliffe, for example, displayed not only Llewellyn but also George Gunn, Cecil Parkin and Tommy Oates, the Nottinghamshire wicketkeeper who was credited with possession of the bandiest legs in county cricket. Every club in the League had players with first-class experience and gate receipts presumably justified professional fees.

Llewellyn seen on the field became Llewellyn pursued in research. I found him in *Wisden* as a player for South Africa, for Hampshire and nearly for England. He was born in Natal and his cricketing talents attracted English attention during tours of South Africa led by Lord Hawke in 1895 and 1898. Llewellyn was recommended to Hampshire, who invited him to England for county qualification by residence, and in 1901 he entered his first full season of English cricket.

His success was immediate and over a period of ten years he was Hampshire's principal all-rounder. In 1902 he was in such impressive form that the England selectors included him among the fourteen players summoned to Edgbaston for the Test against Australia. Qualifications for national teams were less stringently defined then than they are now and Llewellyn would have been acceptable as an England player by the custom and opinion of the time.

In the event he never did play for England but he went back to South Africa to play in Tests of 1902–3 against Australia, and when he left Hampshire, in disagreement over terms of re-engagement, he joined the South African team touring Australia.

In England he turned to League cricket, emerging, by courtesy of Accrington, to help South Africa during the Triangular

Tournament of 1912. That waterlogged series ended Llewellyn's first-class career. He played the remainder of his cricket as a League professional and so, at Undercliffe in the grimy city of Bradford, stepped on a pedestal of which he was never aware.

In my hero-worship of Llewellyn I neither sought nor contemplated a personal association. I watched Undercliffe cricket from distant benches or from the grass at the boundary edge. As far as I know I never saw Llewellyn except when he was in flannels and had there been an equivalent of the modern 'fan-club' I doubt if I should have joined to drool over domestic details. My devotion was to Charles Bennett Llewellyn, cricketer.

To permit assumption of identity in play I had to overcome technical anomalies by ignoring them. I could be Llewellyn batting and bowling without having to be left-handed, as he was. I could be Llewellyn a South African without forfeit of my Yorkshire birthright. I could serve Undercliffe on the playing fields of Heaton—such are the freedoms of childhood's imaginative living.

Llewellyn was a spin bowler of slow-medium pace. His action, as I recall it, was in the orthodox mould with smooth approach, delivery and follow-through, the arm classically high. From dubious hindsight and inadmissible hearsay evidence I have an impression that Llewellyn was an early bowler of the 'chinaman', but the only photographs I know suggest orthodox spin, so perhaps I have misunderstood, or the occasional chinaman was simply an indulgence of Llewellyn's momentary fancy.

Wilfred Rhodes, in the last year of his long life, could not recall Llewellyn's chinamen. He remembered him as an orthodox spinner among Hampshire all-rounders, looking 'like a rather sunburned English player'.

Certainly my youthful and starry eyes would not have discerned spin to be defined. When I watched Llewellyn bowl I was waiting for batsmen to stumble in confusion and for wickets to fall. How he held the ball and which way he spun it from his fingers would have been beyond my observation and probably my comprehension. When I watched Llewellyn bat I anticipated fours and sixes, not every ball, but generously interspersed among defensive compulsions. The expectation was romantic more than rational, but Llewellyn was, in fact, a forceful batsman by inclination.

I have no tangible souvenirs of Llewellyn in the period of my enchantment, no newspaper cuttings, no photographs. My Llewellyn was not measured then and is not remembered now in terms of runs scored and bowling analyses. Details of performance are obscure now through the passing of time and were obscured then by the shimmering haze of admiration. An early dismissal, an expensive and unrewarded bowling spell must have been a disappointment, but such concessions to the nature of cricket never even scratched the surface of childhood faith and loyalty. Llewellyn with a duck and 'none for plenty' was in no danger of dethronement; his failures would have some explanation in misfortune.

He could, for example, be excused dismissal shortly after hitting a six on an occasion at Lidget Green. He would be feeling upset. His straight drive carried not only the boundary line and the seating but also a stone wall, some twelve or fifteen feet high, separating the cricket ground from a main roadway.

Six-hits into the road were uncommon but far from unknown and the players on the field seemed surprised when the return of the ball was long delayed. Eventually came signals and shouts from spectators near the ball and Llewellyn threw down his bat, ran from the crease to the wall and, still padded and gloved, scrambled over and dropped into the roadway.

Information circulated that the ball had pitched in a perambulator occupied by a baby and being pushed along the pavement by the child's mother. In remarkable escape neither child nor mother had been touched by the ball, but of course, Llewellyn could not be expected to hit any more sixes that day—not in my estimation.

The wind's will that is a boy's will never blew Llewellyn out of my favour and my gratitude. He gave an inspiration and it stayed with the picture of shirt-sleeves rolled down for batting, of cap always worn for both batting and bowling, of a creaminess of flannels against whiteness of pads and boots. Llewellyn was a tidy-looking cricketer, of medium height, sturdily built; he was dark-eyed and dark-skinned and South Africans called him coloured.

2. Controversy in Colour

Some sixty years after Llewellyn another South African came to England as a professional cricketer in search of scope and advancement. Llewellyn could and did play for South Africa but had he stayed in that country his first-class experience would have suffered shortfall in quantity. B.L.D'Oliveira's cricket could never have reached first-class status and quality had he not left his native land.

As a coloured South African D'Oliveira was debarred under apartheid law from South African national teams containing white players. In his homeland there were clubs he could not join simply because of his colour, grounds on which he could not play, organizations he could not represent. The principle of separate development determined his boundaries.

In a romance of emigration, made possible by helping hands from overseas and from his own people, D'Oliveira rose to county and international cricket in England. He brought a raw talent and uncommon resolution. He justified himself and his advocates and after six years at league and county level he played for England, thereby stirring implications too intriguing to be overlooked.

The possibilities simmered for two years. D'Oliveira stayed in the England team through 1967 and he toured the West Indies with M.C.C. in the winter of 1967–8. In 1968 Australia were the visitors to England and after the home season M.C.C. were due to send a side to South Africa.

On estimates of cricketing ability D'Oliveira was a candidate for this team, but not an unquestionable selection. Neither his medium-pace bowling nor his middle-order batting had found much success in the West Indies and after England had been heavily defeated in the opening match against Australia D'Oliveira was not invited to the second, third and fourth Tests. Early-season speculation over consequences of D'Oliveira as an England player in South Africa had largely withered when prospects for the tour were being discussed in mid-August. Any awkwardness seemed to have settled itself, purely on playing considerations.

In a week the whole situation turned turtle. D'Oliveira was brought into the Oval Test as a substitute, played an innings of 158, took a timely wicket in a dramatic England victory and so restored himself to the sporting headlines of the world.

At the appointed hour the touring team for South Africa was announced—without D'Oliveira. Reception was predictably controversial and impassioned. The selectors were accused of either political cowardice or myopic cricketing judgement; they were, alternatively, commended for diplomatic discretion or balanced assessment of evidence derived from more than one match. Thinking back, I believe that most of us without direct involvement in politics or touring were prepared to accept the selectors at face value. There was a case for choosing D'Oliveira; there was a case for his omission. As a player he had risen to a specific occasion; as a player he had been unsuccessful on tour in the West Indies and had not held an England place throughout the latest Test series. 'Hard luck, Dolly—but there is always hard luck for someone' would have summed up majority opinion in cricket.

There was, of course, vociferous opinion outside cricket. Dedicated opponents of the South African government were not likely to believe that the M.C.C. selectors had escaped pressure from political agencies. M.C.C. administration was called to the bar for arraignment at a requisitioned Special General Meeting, where the protest was heard sympathetically but its demands rejected. Anti-apartheid organizations, genuine or dubious in underlying motive, made the most of the opportunity.

There was opportunity also in the field of commercial

enterprise. A Sunday newspaper promptly commissioned D'Oliveira to undertake the tour as a cricket correspondent, proclaiming altruism and public service though, naturally, without emphasizing the journalistic limitations of the recruit. D'Oliveira, well aware of the social restrictions that would fall on him and his associates in South Africa, accepted the engagement.

Before he could embark on that forlorn undertaking the situation became further bedevilled. One of the selected players for the tour was found to be medically unfit and the replacement named was D'Oliveira.

The decision doomed the tour. The South African government rejected D'Oliveira as a member of the team, claiming that his ultimate selection represented a deliberate and politically inspired attempt to embarrass the South African government. M.C.C., insisting on the right of choice for their own teams, notified cancellation of the tour. Neither cricketers nor correspondents went to South Africa.

M.C.C. and the South African Cricket Association remained on speaking terms and looked hopefully to a South African tour in England, proposed for 1970.

Expression of this hope was forthcoming from the Cricket Council which replaced M.C.C. as cricket's guardian and guiding light in England. The graceful M.C.C. abdication from responsibilities voluntarily assumed was essentially a concession to the growing commercialization of the game. Cricket was told that M.C.C. as a private club could not be granted public money that might otherwise become available for cricket's general benefit. A nationally representative Cricket Council was recognizable as a concern for the Ministry of Sport and cricket duly doffed its cap of independence.

Old M.C.C. and new Cricket Council were of like mind in attitude towards South African apartheid and South African cricket. They condemned apartheid in principle and in practice and they reserved the right of cricketers to play with or against whom they chose under the protection of the laws of the land.

No one denied that right. In all the protest, persuasion and pressures raised against the tour the logic of cricketing freedom was not challenged. It could not be challenged because it is fundamental in the conception of sporting purpose.

Opponents of the tour were compelled to establish argument on other principles and some of them were prepared to adapt principles to convenience. When argument failed physical force was threatened and organized to bolster persuasion. Cricket pitches and other property of private clubs were damaged and defiled.

The differing tunes of objection created cacophony as preparation for the tour advanced. The complication of issues brought a hardening conviction that concern for the deprived coloured cricketers of South Africa was not the only driving force of the protesters. In several instances self-interest seemed a long way ahead of self-sacrifice in cricket's cause.

A 'Stop the Tour' committee, inspired by the bitter personal hostility of its chairman towards South Africa's government and promoted by juvenile disrespect for opposing lines of thought, proclaimed objects of active disruption. Cricket matches, they said, would be stopped by such physical means as the ruination of turf, invasion of the playing area and harassment of players. By its activities and clear purpose of self-glorification this organization quickly renounced any hope of general public approval.

A complementary organization designated Fair Cricket Campaign was more divisive of opinion, as it was more balanced in aims and behaviour. It sought to reject a white South African cricket team until South African cricket became racially integrated. The Reverend David Sheppard, in his capacities as both cleric and cricketer, had long advocated such a course and he had emphasized his opinion by refusing to play against teams representing only white cricketers of South Africa. Sheppard and the Fair Cricket campaigners promised massive demonstrations outside the grounds in England where the 1970 South Africans were due to play, with Lord's on the Test match occasion a particular target.

The purpose of protest is publicity—to attract attention. Publicity created tends to become a band-wagon accumulating riders whose concern is not primarily the destination and in this instance the ostensible cause of coloured cricketers in South Africa quickly became obscured in a mist of political opportunism. The Labour Government of the day, trade unions, religious and professional organizations exploited the growing conflagration of controversy to pour petrol rather than water on the flames. The Minister with Responsibility for Sport, Mr Denis Howell, said the South African team of 1970 should stay away from England; the Prime Minister, Mr Harold Wilson, condemned a Cricket Council decision to preserve the tour and he openly approved anti-apartheid demonstrations at centres of cricket.

Cricket's representatives in the form of the Cricket Council stubbornly defended their original position. Their responsibility, they insisted, was to cricket and cricketers and if some cricketers in England wanted to play against some cricketers from South Africa they had every right to do so under legal authority and protection and under the moral principles of the game of cricket.

As summer approached, cricket prepared plans for a siege. The tour programme was shortened; pitch and match protection was devised. Test matches were conceived within a literal barricade of barbed wire.

When disruption threat and political persuasion were seen to be failing governmental force was applied. Cricket Council officials were called to the Home Office and told that, on grounds of public interest, the tour would have to be abandoned. The Cricket Council had finally no option but to obey this instruction and they formally withdrew their invitation to the South African Cricket Association. In midsummer there was a General Election and the Labour Government was thrown from office.

Whatever political consequences derived or may eventually derive from this dramatic page in cricket history, cricket itself suffered enormously. Players of great talent were deprived of opportunity to make their full contribution to the game. Cricket in England could no longer claim to be master in its own household of cricket. The privilege of choice in play was taken from individual cricketers against their wishes. In the minor, but not insignificant, consideration of finance first-class cricket lost heavily, and became more dependent on extraneous support.

In its course and in its outcome I doubt if the whole controversy brought many conversions of basic belief. For my own part I think now as I thought then, that the pulse of provincial cricketing opinion was misread, or misinterpreted, in the fever of metropolitan politics. In my philosophy the conception of apartheid is wholly unacceptable; I count it abhorrent in principle and untenable in the long run of practice. Apartheid and sport are a contradiction in terms.

I do not play games in defence or defiance of apartheid or any form of racial discrimination. I follow games for the satisfactions they bring of themselves and I am prepared to share such satisfactions with anyone of similar outlook, regardless of colour, creed or political persuasion.

I claim no distinction for this outlook. I have found it so general in my sporting sphere that until the Tests of 1968 and 1970 it never required identification or expression. All I asked, as thousands of others asked, was the right to indulge in cricket of agreeable circumstances and companionship.

Challenge to that right, not support for apartheid or any extraneous cause, roused our resentment. We objected strongly to being told with whom we should or must play cricket or not play cricket. We granted the same right to every cricketer. The refusal of David Sheppard and some coloured cricketers employed by English counties to play against white teams from South Africa was appreciated and respected. That was their choice, their privilege of persuasion by example.

Tub-thumping and protest-marching in the anti-apartheid cause could have taken place every day in every part of the country as far as we were concerned, provided these activities were not permitted to interfere with lawful individual pursuits of citizenship. In our view cricket fixtures with the 1970 South African team were legal and they were wanted by some of us. We expected, in a community of freedom claimed by the protesters, to be allowed to go about our lawful business without let or hindrance; to play and attend without physical harassment. Any moral harassment we could deal with in our own consciences.

This opinion I found to be strongly held in provincial cricketing circles. I was in Middlesbrough during a Yorkshire match when a rumour spread, through misinformation from the Press Box, that the Cricket Council had cancelled the tour. Public reaction was promptly expressed in a growl of disapproval from the nearby spectators. The anger was against dictation, against pressures by the organizations of protest. It came from the heart.

In all probability few of the Middlesbrough spectators would have been directly affected by the tour. The South Africans were not due in Middlesbrough and the Headingley Test, threatened with disruption, was seventy miles away. The basic Middlesbrough feeling, plainly and luridly expressed, was that cricket had been 'let down' and that forces of law and order had been defeated.

On this day the Cricket Council had not, in fact, conceded the tour. They had repelled boarders, for the last time, and replaced political responsibility where it belonged. If government could not assure peaceful and practical cricket within the law it must say so and acknowledge its incapacity. It did, and the whole country duly took note for future reference.

The consequences of political influence in sport are beyond precise expression but not beyond conjecture. Their manifestation is all too evident. An athletics inadequacy has brought governmental reproof; a sporting occasion has served as setting for political fanaticism extending to murder. The independence of sport is everywhere becoming a sacrifice on the altar of subsidy.

Quietly and firmly and no doubt over a long period I hope and believe that sport will reject bondage and preserve the truth in itself. Sport without freedom to be sport of its own choice is no sport at all. Its discipline must always be the self-discipline of voluntary and devoted disciples to an art. It is one of man's stairways to the stars.

3. Two Tommies

Tommy Birtles and Tommy Gill were servants and masters of the Barnsley Cricket Club I knew when I was growing through school and undergraduate years. They were employees in the sense that they were paid weekly wages and subject to engagement and dismissal by the club committee; they were independent authorities by virtue of their undisputed craftsmanship.

T.J.Birtles was deprived of a chance to establish himself in first-class cricket. He played for Yorkshire in 1913 and 1914, with promise rather than convincing performance, but the interruption of war precluded development in critical years. When county cricket came back in 1919 Birtles was thirty-one years old, approaching middle age in agility and needing a spectacular re-entry to justify extension of a career never advanced beyond tentative beginnings. Birtles had made a century against Lancashire in 1914 but nine innings for Yorkshire in 1919 brought him only 113 runs.

At club level he was an impressive batsman. The Barnsley of the 1920s carried repute as a strong side in the highest grouping of the Yorkshire Council and Birtles, as match professional, was the foundation of their batting. He scored readily and he scored heavily, once, at least, to the extent of 1000 runs in a season's programme of Council matches.

The features of his batsmanship were late cutting and skilful on-side placing. His preliminary movement contained a short, straight back-lift and a slight advancement of the left foot, so that when he played the forward defensive stroke he seemed to take two steps with his left foot. To my schoolboy eyes he looked 'professional'. I could appreciate his dismissal by l.b.w. decision; I could understand that he might be beaten and bowled, but I should have been astonished and offended to see a mishit ballooning into the covers. I cannot remember that I ever did; the crudities of batsmanship were not in him.

On the field he had that 'first-class' appearance deriving from accoutrement as well as from methods of play. His flannels, pads, gloves and cap looked like a standard uniform as distinct from improvisations for a leisure occupation. He was dressed as a cricketer rather than being dressed to play cricket.

His cap was a faded blue and was worn with the 'set' of long usage. His pads were personal property, rather broader than the general pattern and with a tendency to floppiness above the knee. They were as much a part of his character at the crease as trousers with an ample seat and a cream-coloured shirt.

Differences in appearance between the casual player and what might be termed the practising cricketer are not, in fact, illusory. The casual tends to equip himself by chance purchase, made under necessity. He needs a shirt so he buys a white one from an outfitter's shop, and as likely as not it will be made of cotton. The cricketer constantly in activity turns to material essentially woollen. The club cricketer often bats in pads provided from the communal store and, using a different pair each week, gives none a chance to appear tailor-made.

Tommy Birtles, playing club cricket for Barnsley, reminded me of the county cricketers I had seen at Park Avenue, Headingley, Bramall Lane and Scarborough. He looked his part. As the professional he was accorded little privileges, such as a particular peg for his clothes in the dressing-room, a recognized position in the batting order and the choice of station in the field.

I cannot remember his ever going in anywhere but first and I cannot remember him in any fielding position that involved a likelihood of having to run after the ball. At this stage of his career Tommy Birtles was not built for running. At the wicket he made his skill in placing and his experience save his legs. He could contrive singles at a trot for himself, but he was disinclined to scamper on his partner's behalf. You were permitted to lead him in the scoring, provided you made most of your runs in boundaries.

He was a careful calculator on grounds where the scoreboard showed only the total. Through his longest innings he would keep his own score and his partners were duly warned of impending achievement. 'I'm forty-nine,' he would murmur in mid-wicket conference, 'I'll be pushing a single next over. Get ready.'

In Barnsley legends grew around him, based on his recognized prowess at the crease and on his capacity for anecdote and recollection in the dressing-room. His was the story of the young miner turned professional footballer who was taken for his first stay in an hotel and had seven helpings of soup at dinner because he was unaware that other courses would follow.

Birtles featured himself in recollection of a wet 'Feast', which is the local holiday week. For Feast week Barnsley usually arranged three home Council matches and on the first day of one holiday programme Birtles and the wicketkeeper were walking together through the town on their way to the Shaw Lane ground. As they passed a butcher's shop the wicketkeeper asked Birtles to 'wait a minute; I'll just get my steak'.

The raw steak was wanted by the wicketkeeper to serve as padding for the palm of his gloves but on this occasion the day turned wet and the match was abandoned without Barnsley being required to take a turn in the field. As the players were dispersing the wicketkeeper, who was an undomesticated bachelor, said to Birtles: 'Here, you might as well have this steak.'

On the second day the customary wicketkeeping preparations were undertaken but again the weather prohibited cricket and Birtles took home steak. On the way to the third match the wicketkeeper was checked as he entered the butcher's shop. Birtles looked at the watery sky and then at the butcher's display counter. 'Get chops,' he said. 'We're tired of steak'.

Batting success for Birtles was a consequence of sound method, but scope for exposition was widened by the work of Tommy Gill, Barnsley's groundsman, a professional.

The two Tommies, contemporary in service at Shaw Lane for at least a decade, were directly contrasting in appearance, function and outlook. Birtles had a well-padded figure and was rather pale in complexion, never tanning deeply. Gill was lean to a point of emaciation and his face, neck and forearms were burned brick-red. Birtles was a batsman. Gill was a bowler, right-arm, of medium pace; he was trustworthy in length and direction, but he had no specific quality to induce outstanding analyses.

Saturday after Saturday he would open the Barnsley bowling and take his two for thirty-four in twelve overs. He must, of course, have known some days of notably greater success or failure but in memory—affectionate memory—he stays close to his average performance, his skill and industry as a groundsman restricting his opportunities as a bowler. He rarely allowed himself, or anybody else, a chance to decimate a batting side of Council quality at Shaw Lane.

His pride was in a perfection of pitches. They were essentially hand-made with water and roller. No doubt Tommy Gill was versed in deployment of fertilizers and dressings and tricks of his trade, but he made roller and mowing-machine his basic tools.

I never knew the terms of his engagement, but he could not have been paid on time rates. No club could have afforded him by such reckoning. His working hours were from an unspecified and unobserved early morning to the end of daylight and he spent no time in going to his nearby house for lunch and tea. He brought those meals with him and he ate them in his machine-store, gaining privacy if not the most salubrious of surroundings.

When I first knew the Barnsley Cricket Club Tommy Gill was as established as the pavilion and the tiered enclosure and the smooth playing area. He was there, a part of the scene.

In the earliest of my recollections he is leading the horse and the shafted heavy roller round and round the outfield or across and across the 'middle', progress slow and stately. For outfield-cutting the horse was on reins of rope and Tommy Gill steered the cutter as he walked behind it. For pitch preparation he pushed a closely set hand-mower. My summer picture of Shaw Lane has a background of Tommy Gill ceaselessly cutting and rolling—and walking, walking, walking.

When the last of the horses died, or was superannuated, the club bought a motor-mower and Tommy Gill changed from groom to mechanic. I gathered he preferred the horse as less temperamental than the machine, but he attended to both with the same placid persistence. The motor-mower had a detachable seat from which driving and cutting control could be maintained and which was intended to save the groundsman's legs if not to represent the acme of riding comfort. 'I don't think that will be used much,' was Gill's conclusion after demonstration of the driving seat; he walked behind the petrol engine as he had walked behind the horse.

In my years at Barnsley Tommy Gill's pattern of working attire never changed. He wore a khaki shirt, cavalry riding breeches, thick woollen stockings and boots. His hat was a tribly of indefinable colour, with the unbound brim turned down all the way round. Both at work and at play—which was a variation of work—he was impeccably neat in appearance. His flannels, worn only for matches, were always carefully pressed and he rolled up his shirt-sleeves in precise folds. His cricket boots, lovingly preserved, gleamed whiteness and his was the bag that carried a spare lace for emergencies.

His summer routine was groundsman's work, unassisted,

through morning and afternoon and net practice supervision in the evening. Practices began when sufficient players had assembled to provide a batsman, a batsman-in-waiting and three bowlers and when Tommy Gill decided that his meagre tea had been digested. Practice did not begin without the presence of Tommy Gill.

Before cricket there was rolling of the two net pitches and reluctant rollers therefore had to decide between the early arrival that meant an early innings with rolling duties or later arrival that gave escape from rolling but an innings delayed at the risk of failing light and lack of bowling. Custom rather than law governed the practice procedure. If Tommy Birtles wanted to bat he took first innings as a professional privilege; thereafter the batting order was by time of arrival, with occasional delicate direction to accommodate the hierarchy. Perhaps three times in a season Tommy Gill claimed an innings, but it was a rare night when he did not bowl for at least half an hour.

His net bowling was as studious as his match endeavour, though his concern was much more for the behaviour of the practice pitches than for any demonstration of his playing talent. He was horrified by any sign of the ball lifting unexpectedly and he always tried to site the nets so that the ball was pitching on a down-slope rather than an up-slope.

Tommy Gill was rarely seen in idleness. When wet weather kept him indoors he would be cleaning and repairing club bats and pads, or sweeping out the dressing-rooms, or investigating some mechanical mystery. The extent of his labours was discovered in the summer he was attacked and very nearly defeated by pneumonia. The club survived and fulfilled all cricketing obligations, but desperate improvisations and vast volunteer forces were needed.

Tommy Birtles went from Barnsley to be coach at Gresham's School, Holt, and the last time I saw him was during a Nottinghamshire and Yorkshire match at Trent Bridge. We met near George Parr's tree, which commemorates another strong on-side batsman. Tommy Gill went on bowling, for fun or from habit, long after he had left the Barnsley club, and to keep himself in a sufficiency of daily walking he became greenkeeper to a municipal golf club. His cricket was reproduced in a son with a bowling action exactly like that of his father. Tommy Birtles had a daughter who, of course, married a Barnsley cricketer.

4. Bramall Lane

To claim that I knew Bramall Lane as a cricket ground for more than sixty years would be stretching the meaning of words, but there is factual accuracy in saying that I attended cricket at Bramall Lane from 1909 to 1973. In 1909 I was a babe in arms, taken to Bramall Lane because my father was playing there; in 1973 Bramall Lane ceased to be a cricket ground.

Before I could distinguish between a pavilion enclosure and a playpen the family home moved from Sheffield to Bradford, so my first understanding of Bramall Lane derived from *Wisden*'s and my father's reminiscence. I knew the flavour before I enjoyed the taste.

The eventual recognition was remarkably like the mental picture and the years of the First World War scarcely changed the outline presented by pre-war photographs I had seen. In my youthful excursions to Bramall Lane from outside Sheffield I went by train and followed the crowd, on foot, from station to ground. The admission gate was where I expected it to be, my money or my credentials seemed acceptable and beyond the enclosing rails stretched the turf of promised land requiring no adjustment of preconception. Considering the matter at all, I should no doubt have satisfied myself that this was Bramall Lane as it always had been and would continue to be. I was much more concerned with the batting and bowling than with the buildings, and simply accepted Bramall Lane as a place where Yorkshire and other teams played cricket.

This acceptance stayed with me through widening aesthetic experience. I have never been appalled, mystified, enchanted or amused, as others have been, by the sight of cricket in a Bramall Lane setting. I can understand varied reactions, parti-

C

cuarly in relation to the decades of 1950 and 1960 when Bramall Lane had become a manifest anachronism. A first sight of it on a wet or merely overcast Wednesday might well raise alarm and despondency; it could certainly seem a sick joke that anyone should want to play cricket in a pit of concrete and steel, with the evening shadow of a football stand putting half the outfield in blackness and even encroaching on the pitch.

In its last years of cricket Bramall Lane had ceased to look like a cricket ground with adaptations for football. It did not look like a football ground, either. It must have looked, on first sight, like nothing on earth.

Because I had known Bramall Lane all my life and had absorbed its changes year by year I was neither shocked nor sentimentally dismayed by its ultimate reconstitution. In commercial sport a Bramall Lane trying to serve both cricket and football had no chance of survival. As a joint accommodation it was only half a football ground and a travesty of a field for cricket.

That there should be no Bramall Lane in cricket was a saddening thought; that a Bramall Lane long known and respected should have lost character and quality was wistful reflection; but that Bramall Lane as last seen in cricket had any claim to preservation outside the history books made no argument for me.

Within the history books Bramall Lane holds a high rating. It was as familiar in cricket as Old Trafford or The Oval and as personalized as Lord's. Cricketers the world over are familiar with the name of Bramall Lane and thousands who have never been there carry a firm impression of the place and of its people.

This character derived from history and crystallized in the twenty years before 1914 and the twenty years between the Great Wars. Bramall Lane was created essentially for cricket by enterprising cricketers. In 1855, when it was rented from the Duke of Norfolk, it was a field among fields on the outskirts of commercial and industrial Sheffield. Heavy steel manufacturing was concentrated in the Don valley with the lighter cutlery and tool-making factories scattered along the banks of the Sheaf.

From commercial Sheffield ran a country lane to the file-factory and adjoining residence of David Brammall and the Brammall's Lane of conversational usage became Bramall Lane as a thoroughfare and as the identification of a field enclosed for cricket and other sports in 1855. When the ninety-nine-year lease of the paddock was under discussion its advantage in 'being free from smoke' was emphasized and its usage was conditional on cricket matches being 'conducted in a respectable manner'.

Cricket in the middle of the nineteenth century was an expanding game and an increasing public entertainment. It had emerged from a tawdry period of betting and bribery to become a socially accredited pastime for amateur players and a widening opportunity for professionals. Michael J. Ellison and his fellow promoters wanted Bramall Lane for the betterment of their own cricket and needed the promotion of Bramall Lane to justify its existence and develop its potentiality. Within a decade of taking the ground they had established the Yorkshire County Cricket Club.

Bramall Lane and Yorkshire cricket grew up together. Yorkshire cricket was never confined to Sheffield nor was it supplied with playing resources predominantly from Sheffield; but for forty years it was governed from Sheffield and Bramall Lane was its spiritual home.

The ultimate in cricket ground honour was accorded in 1902 when England met Australia in the third Test of the series. The accolade was mistimed. It came too late if Bramall Lane were to be considered as an attractive setting for cricket; too soon if financial considerations were to be paramount.

By this time the ground had conceded all pastoral pretensions. Houses and paved streets, factories and service industry had covered the neighbouring fields and gardens and, though cricketers were still granted sight of the sky, no tree, no vegetation except the playing lawn, soothed the roving eye. Bramall Lane provided cricket—and Association football in the winter—to watch, but little else for inspiring contemplation. Its origins had been completely obscured.

As a commercial arena its potential was still unfulfilled. It could accommodate enormous crowds, but not in any great creature comfort or with appropriate financial return. In 1898 management and ownership had changed into the form of a limited company, with freehold purchased and funds allocated for ground development. The Test match came before the development could be completed.

Bramall Lane's first and last Test match was full of disappointment for the England team and the Sheffield authorities. Australia won the game and the public reaction to the occasion was discouraging. A total attendance of 40,000 over three days was far below expectations and receipts were reduced by lack of stand seats to be sold. The early July weather—of a notoriously rainy summer—was damp and gloomy and play was harassed by showers and light so poor as to create a lasting reputation. Bramall Lane had to confess a failure.

It knew success at county level and preserved it for fifty years. Bramall Lane spectators rejoiced in Yorkshire's cricket before and between the wars and developed a character that was both fascinating and forbidding. Bramall Lane came to epitomize a Southern conception of Northern cricket that was acceptable, because beneficial, to cricketers of the North; if visiting teams felt strangely circumstanced in the grey of stone and steel they might lose a wicket or two or drop a catch before they became acclimatized. If the rough humour of the watching thousands seemed difficult to understand and liable to misinterpretation a temperamental weakness might be exposed to Yorkshire's advantage.

Throughout the cricket world Bramall Lane grew synonymous with smoky skies and biting comment. The characteristics were exaggerated from a foundation on fact. Sheffield skies were smoky and Sheffield wit was incisive, but, of course, there were sunny days to help the batsmen and reproof was directed on friend as well as on foe. Bramall Lane could praise or plague with some approach to impartiality, though it would be true enough to say that the visitor usually had to overcome an initial prejudice applied against any stranger or challenger.

One evening in the 1920s I paid my shilling to take a place in the 'Grinder's Stand', which was the seating on the Bramall Lane side of the ground. Sussex had been dismissed and Yorkshire had to meet Maurice Tate with the new ball for an hour or so before close of play. Tate, bowling from the pavilion end, was in magnificent form but completely out of luck. He beat both Holmes and Sutcliffe and shaved the stumps; he had each batsman palpably missed by the wicketkeeper, who was playfully strangled at the end of the over. Tate's bowling was worth three or four wickets and he took none, but he was honoured by the 'Grinders'.

Holmes and Sutcliffe won applause for their scoring strokes and acclamation when their partnership reached fifty (in less than an hour), but Tate was acknowledged at the end of every splendid over and his performance was the talking point of the day, though there was nothing to show for it in his analysis.

That was the personification of Bramall Lane, the distinction of its 'shilling' spectators. Of course they relished records, of course they were delighted by Yorkshire success and the downfall of opponents, of course they wore hearts of loyalty on their sleeves, but they were knowledgeable enough to recognize outstanding cricket from any source. Bramall Lane may not have been able to sustain the presentation of Test cricket, but it subjected every match and every player to a test of its own devising and awarded unfading 'caps' of acclaim or humiliation.

The traditional Bramall Lane crowd was not representative of Sheffield alone. Spectators flocked in from the city and its suburbs but they came also from Rotherham and Doncaster and Barnsley and all the townships of South Yorkshire. They came by train and tram and bus and they claimed Bramall Lane as theirs in Yorkshire cricket.

Assembly was part of the day's excitement. The railway 'cricket ticket' filled the local trains; trams and buses ran 'special' services. Along the two approach roads to the city, Bramall Lane and Shoreham Street, pedestrians spilled from pavement into roadway, reducing the traffic flow to their own pace. Raincoat and lunch-box, in one form or another, made a uniform and the first sight of a turnstile queue inspired a hastening stride.

Inside the ground disposition was hierarchical. County and local club members with pavilion and enclosure privilege were invariably established hours before the start of play. These were, so to speak, the occupational followers of cricket, practised in finding favoured seats and in guarding possession against all-comers. Their characteristic accoutrement included raincoat, rug or cushion and refreshments carrier. These were the avid newspaper and brochure readers, the self-appointed authorities on dressing-room and committee intimacies. They knew Herbert Sutcliffe's batting average and the colour of his motor-car. Among themselves they were severe critics of Yorkshire performances, but they tolerated no denigration by 'lesser breeds without the law'.

Opposite the pavilion ran the long football stand, raised above concrete terracing. Here the seating was slightly more comfortable than in the pavilion enclosure, but the cricket was only distantly in view and a sense of isolation was discouragingly strong.

The 'popular' sides of the ground gave witness to cricket's fascination and spectatorial hardihood. The Grinder's Stand had wooden seating but on the Shoreham Street side the embankment, which was primarily a football service, offered only concrete steps and iron crush barriers. A day's cricket was a day's endurance.

From discomfort and devotion the Bramall Lane crowd originated a world-wide reputation for sharp wit and shrewd comment. At its best the expression of opinion was pointed without being offensive. Rebuke was for the misdemeanour rather than for the perpetrator and the same player could experience condemnation and acclaim on the same afternoon. Judgement, on the whole, was equitable and Bramall Lane knew cricket as well as the game can be known from an on-looker's viewpoint.

Occasionally there was misinterpretation and consequent misbehaviour. Disrespect towards the umpires led to an M.C.C. inquiry in 1924 and a threat by Middlesex to refuse further fixtures with Yorkshire. Patriotic fervour once or twice stepped beyond the bounds of good humour, but few cricketers, from any part of the world, counted playing at Bramall Lane an experience better to be avoided.

In the 1930s particularly, the cricket itself assumed a characteristic pattern based on the qualities in the pitch and the features of the enclosure. First mornings were frequently found to be helpful to swing bowling and a batting struggle could be expected until lunch-time. When early moisture had gone from turf and atmosphere the conditions eased to encourage high scoring and remained, in fine weather, favourable to batsmen for the rest of the match.

In persistent dampness swing bowlers could keep their authority and first-morning drama spread into second and third days, as in that memorable match between Yorkshire and the 1938 Australians when Bowes, for the only time in his career, had conditions to his liking in bowling to Bradman. A comparable engagement of abiding memory came later when Trueman and May met as protagonists for their counties.

Bramall Lane was buffeted by German raiders in the Second World War and the years following saw its gradual decline as a stately home of cricket. The physical ravages of war, in which both turf and stands were damaged, remained in evidence long after war had ended and the reconstruction of the stands was more beneficial to football than to cricket.

Spiritual restoration was never accomplished. Sheffield shared the booming public interest in cricket revived, but, when the first-class game began to lose some of its quality in the 1950s and Yorkshire was not the champion county in a period of ten years, Bramall Lane illustrated the decline. Crowds became smaller and noticeably less knowledgeable. The famed comment of tradition degenerated to myopic crudity. Character took on the shoddy appearance of the property. Bramall Lane could not live for ever on a reputation created in a different age.

For me the inevitable ending was engraved one afternoon of interrupted play. On the Shoreham Street embankment a few spectators, dispersed in groups, waited for a possible return of the players. The air was damp, the skies were grey and a melancholy inconsequence pervaded the whole scene.

On the embankment a solitary youth occupied himself with kicking an empty beer-can from top to bottom of the concrete terracing. He followed the can to the lowest step, took a hand from his pocket, picked up the can and threw it back towards the top of the terracing. He climbed the steps and set the can rolling down again. When it stopped he kicked it—tinkle, tinkle, tinkle.

He repeated the exercise a dozen times and more, the irritating jangle echoing through the cavernous emptiness. Nobody attempted to stop him, nobody offered rebuke. Bramall Lane had reached a resignation of spirit.

Within ten years the cricket turf was torn away. Bramall Lane could no longer justify a cricketing existence, but it has, at least, left a name and a memory beyond obliteration.

Wilfred Rhodes – 4187 wickets, 39 802 runs and all the wisdom of cricket. *Below right*: F. E. Woolley, devastator of fast bowling.

Top, left: D. G. Bradman, phenomenon of batting.
Top, right: W. R. Hammond in classical finish to the drive.
Below: Triumvirate of Greatness – Hedley Verity, Herbert Sutcliffe and Maurice Leyland, contemporary in Yorkshire and England teams.

L. Hutton – master of technique, knighted for services to cricket.

Top, left: K. R. Miller, Australian of inspiration.
Top right: P. B. H. May, captain of Surrey and England and a model of modesty and batsmanship. *Below*: Learie Constantine, Frank Worrell and Ted Dexter – three great players who were thrilling to watch.

5. The Modest Cricketer

Of all the cricketers I have known on first-class fields the one with the least inclination towards delusions of personal grandeur was Cyril Turner. He played for Yorkshire over a period of twenty-one seasons, shared in triumphs unparalleled in cricket history, and never ceased to deprecate his own significance or to wonder how he came to be in such illustrious company.

There was no affectation in his diffidence. He simply did not aspire to the individual greatness that he recognized in the leading players of his team and he was genuinely grateful for the chance to associate with them and to be able to live a life of cricket.

He waited a long time for the ultimate satisfactions. In his first nine seasons of county experience he was granted only thirty-one innings and 314 overs and he took part in more matches as twelfth man than as one of the eleven. He was a thoroughly professional twelfth man, not in the sense of requiring pay, but in awareness of obligation and concentration on the business in hand. With Turner in the dressing-room one signal from the field was enough for a wanted cap or sweater. When a substitute fieldsman was needed Turner was not only promptly available but competent wherever he was placed.

After the waiting years Turner slipped unobtrusively into a powerful team to give it greater strength. His function was that of comprehensive insurance or the supplementary braking systems in high-quality cars.

As an established player Turner was neither a leading batsman nor an essential bowler. In the routine stretches of Yorkshire's programme he was the handyman, not to say the dogsbody. As a batsman following Sutcliffe, Hutton, Mitchell, Leyland, Barber and sometimes Yardley there was usually not much left for him to do. As a medium-pace seam bowler he was not a competing factor in a side containing Bowes, Smailes, Verity and either Macaulay or Ellis Robinson.

As he had waited on the fringe of the team in case convenience or emergency required him to play, so, when he was in the team, he waited to serve for convenience or in emergency. In the Yorkshire batting Turner was first choice for nightwatchman. In the bowling he delivered the over to permit a change of ends or he filled the gap until circumstances became favourable for another bowler.

These modest services were undertaken with the same unfailing sense of responsibility that was shown on the more demanding occasions of emergency. Turner as a nightwatchman dismissed in the day's last minutes would have been his own sternest judge. If his change-ends over yielded runs he felt a sense of failure.

Emergencies that brought him from his customary obscurity to prominence were teams depleted or the occasional crises inherent in cricket. When leading batsmen were away Turner became a leading batsman, number three in the order or even opening the innings. When the regular new-ball bowlers were unavailable Turner took the new ball.

He was trustworthy in either capacity. He was not a dominating batsman or gifted technically and temperamentally to force a way to distinction, but he was not out of his element batting high in the order. He was unlikely to stir the imagination with any sweetness of touch or flourish of stroke, but he would certainly not offend the eye with crudities of execution. Turner was left-handed; he crouched a little in his stance; his movements were inclined to be abbreviated rather than flowing, but his bat was commendably straight and his drive was deceptively powerful.

His bowling had the same virtues and limitations as his

batting. It was modest in range of endeavour, orthodox in conception and serviceable rather than exciting. Turner bowled right-arm at medium pace with the slightly open-chested action that heralds inswing. The inswing was not startling, as by Root or Procter, but it commanded attention and careful length and direction commanded respect; so Turner's bowling was usually economical if not notably profitable.

At first-class level Turner could never have been an outstanding bowler, but his 173 wickets for Yorkshire at a cost of thirty runs each give a false impression of his usefulness. He was rarely given opportunity to bowl to any personal purpose. He went on at the unhelpful end to permit exploitation of the other; he was required to hold scoring in check as major bowling forces were being regrouped; he was often first-change in challenge to skilled batsmen already settled in, but he was rarely, or never, brought back to enjoy plunder among 'nine, ten, jack'.

Conditions suited to his manner of bowling were also advantageous to others with prior claim, so all through his career Turner was deprived of much chance to return the dramatic analysis. Once, at Gloucester, he was offered scope. The day was cloudy, the pitch had the slight softness of early season and a persistent breeze blew from third man. To these encouraging conditions for the inswing bowler was added the bonus of l.b.w. (n), the experimental rule of 1935 that, in course of time, made cricket a duller game to watch, if not to play.

When Yorkshire lost the toss Turner was given the new ball because he and Smailes were the only new-ball bowlers in the side. Smailes and Verity bowled, between them, thirty-seven careful overs downwind and Turner bowled thirty-three overs into the wind to take seven wickets for fifty-four runs. Obligations had been met. Turner had taken his triumph from the course of duty. He neither expected, nor was he accorded, any subsequent priorities in similar circumstances. He was pleased with his performance at Gloucester, not because he thought it might carry him to the threshold of a bowling career, but because he had fulfilled a Yorkshire purpose.

Cyril Turner was uncompromisingly and unalterably loyal to Yorkshire cricket. His was loyalty with open eyes as well as open heart, for he could see and would acknowledge a cricketing error or weakness, but he always sought a compensating strength. Yorkshire might be wrong occasionally, but that was all the more reason to remember how often they were right. The captain might institute some foolhardy practices in the field but he would be first to follow them and that was leadership Turner could support.

Turner did support some breathtaking Yorkshire practices in the field. Under Sellers Yorkshire evolved the piratical field settings that snatched away batting lives with catches in positions yards nearer the crease than was either customary or prudent. The thought of Cyril Turner with a cutlass between his teeth and flaunting the skull and crossbones lays strain on the imagination, but where his leaders went Turner never hesitated to follow. He joined Arthur Mitchell in the gully or in the slips to make such wonderful catches that 'c. Mitchell' was sometimes recorded instinctively before correction to 'c. Turner'. He stood in the leg trap where experience and speed of reaction are safety factors but where good fortune is a man's best friend in escape from injury.

Turner did not escape injury in the leg trap. More than once he had to miss matches for periods of painful convalescence and on his return to the field he knew and his captain knew that further leg-trap fielding would be even more exacting. Turner went back into the leg trap without hesitation and Sellers put him there without comment. This was not bravado on the part of the fieldsman or cruelty on the part of the captain. It was professional acceptance of responsibility by Turner and acknowledgement of that professional attitude by Sellers. Every man in the Yorkshire team appreciated the situation. Nobody said a word about it.

The chance to pay tribute to Turner arose from another injury. Batting at Scarborough Turner had to be taken to hospital after edging the ball into his face in attempting a hook, and from sympathy over the accident the Yorkshire players and supporters could find good reason for expressing compliment without any appearance of patronage. My own reflections on Turner's services in cricket chanced to appear in the *Yorkshire Post* one day during a match at Leicester, where team and travelling Press were staying in the same hotel.

When players and writers are on terms of family association congratulations and condemnations tend to be muted or not expressed at all. Hedley Verity no more expected me to say 'wonderful bowling' to him than I expected him to say 'well written' to me.

Custom was set aside in the corridors and lounges of the Stag and Pheasant. Almost without exception the Yorkshire players made a point of approving my little tribute to Turner. 'It is time,' they all said, in one form or another, 'that Cyril got some notice; he's earned it.'

Turner was characteristically grateful for appreciation and good wishes, but he was also slightly apprehensive.

'Am I finishing, then?' he asked.

'Finishing, Cyril? Certainly not. What makes you think that?'

'Well, I thought people said nice things about you only when you retired.'

The nice things of retirement came Turner's way at the end of the 1946 season, though in departure as in activity he was not given the centre of the stage. He left the Yorkshire first team at the same time as Leyland and Barber and in a period of severely rationed newsprint the hail and farewell could not do justice to all—if, indeed, to any.

Turner retreated quietly from the championship fields, but he did not retire from cricket or from Yorkshire service. In an appointment as senior professional he became mentor to second-team captain and players and from club cricket at

Sheffield he heralded incipient greatness seen in a teenage fast bowler named Trueman.

At the end of playing days Turner became Yorkshire's scorer, thankfully so but unconvinced of his own adequacies. He worried about the neatness of his book; he worried about attitudes of irresponsibility, incomprehensible to him, that he observed in a new generation of cricketers, but to be 'in cricket' was a satisfaction he sought to preserve through a period of deteriorating health.

During his last season as a player he had taken to wearing glasses and in his term as scorer he became increasingly subject to severe headaches. The summer travel and the concentration required in the scorer's box eventually became too burdensome to bear, but it was only under insistence in the guise of a command that he allowed himself to be taken home early from a match at Worcester.

Turner passed his closing years in poor health and died at the age of sixty-six. In his own estimation his was no more than a reflected glory, but even on that assessment the mirror was kept clear by pride of service.

6. *Days Remembered*

'Days Remembered' was the general title given to a winter cricket series in the *Yorkshire Post*. The original request by the Sports Editor was for recollection of notable matches I had seen, but the space available would have necessitated a factual rather than a personal recall of whole matches. I found, also, rather to my surprise, that I did not remember many matches in their entirety or for their own sake.

In cricket more than in most games the result, the overall attainment, the impact of success and failure seem secondary to the moments and means encountered in the course of construction. A magnificent first-day innings is in no way diminished because a third-day rainstorm washes away the match into inconsequence. In cricket the incident, the hour, the day can have a life of their own, a complete satisfaction in a match that might itself be incomplete and therefore without fulfilment of character.

Some cricket I do remember in terms of a match as distinct from a batting or bowling performance or an absorbing hour. In the mind's eye I see Yorkshire's sensational defeat by Essex at Huddersfield in 1935 as an entity, though it did extend into two days and did include memorable individual achievements.

I see it as a match of fast bowling, of batting dramatic in either failure or success, of such imbalance in its development that the very one-sidedness was a source of captivation.

The match was contained in four playing sessions of consistent and fair weather. Each session was a section with an identifiable shape that fitted precisely into the ultimate pattern. The whole could be seen in any of the parts, yet assembly had to be complete before the full wonder could be appreciated.

The course of the cricket was simple in definition. On the morning of the first day Yorkshire were all out for thirty-one. In the afternoon Essex thrust aside counter-attack and established advantage which they extended in the evening to a first-innings lead of 303. On the morning of the second day Yorkshire began and ended their second innings, scoring ninety-nine. Before the match began such outcome was beyond contemplation; at the end of it the logic was as discernible as the shock had been stunning.

As I remember events and reactions the Huddersfield spectators were dumbfounded more than dismayed. They could not readily accept the evidence of their own eyes and followers at second-hand certainly complained of misreporting. The atmosphere of incredulity never left the match. There was laughter in the pavilion enclosure as Yorkshire's batsmen hurried by but it was laughter without mirth, a defiance of the fates to inflict any greater pain.

The Huddersfield crowd were not angered by Yorkshire's inefficiency of the hour. There was no loss of confidence, or of pride, in the team, no fear that one failure might be followed by another, season after season, world without end. The composite Yorkshire supporter who sat through the astonishments of Huddersfield's day and a half was surprised and pained but not gloomy.

He—and she—saw the Essex bowling and batting as a thunderbolt from a clear sky, not as the onset of a new ice-age. Yorkshire would be victorious in the next match (as they were) and champions at the end of the season (as they were). It was not disappointing that Yorkshire should be dismissed for totals of thirty-one and ninety-nine where Essex scored 334. It was unbelievable.

Thousands of people did disbelieve the facts. At the ground and in newspaper offices all over the county telephonists were busily responding to callers seeking confirmation or denial of the stop-press scores. Spectators arriving in ignorance shortly before lunch on the first day noted that Essex were batting with very few runs on the board and assumed that the start of the match had been delayed. They regarded the revelations of Yorkshire's downfall as attempted humour in rather poor taste.

Apart from an hour on the first day when Yorkshire took three or four cheap wickets the whole match followed a course dictated by Essex. They gained command, they kept command and they completed conquest.

Interpretation from the bare bones of the scorebook might have suggested a personal exhibition by M.S.Nichols rather than a contest between teams. Nichols bowled unchanged to take four wickets in one innings and seven in the other and he hit two sixes and sixteen fours in his score of 146. This was, of course, one of the great all-round performances of cricket history and Nichols was unquestionably the player of the match, but, curiously enough, he was not a dominant figure in isolation.

He was the most successful bowler and the most successful batsman but he was, in the feeling of the occasion, only characteristic of the bowling and the batting that overwhelmed Yorkshire. He had a bowling partner of even greater pace than himself and in his splendid innings he had one partner who stood with him for three hours.

The negative combined with the positive to create match identity and flavour. Read and Nichols extracted paralysing pace from the pitch; Yorkshire had only Bowes in the classification of fast bowling and he, for once, could not make the most of conditions, which were, in fact, not precisely the same for both sides. Essex bowled in the mornings, Yorkshire in the afternoon—and that can make a significant difference in the height of summer.

In this instance Essex bowled to their opportunities; Yorkshire did not. Essex, mainly through Nichols and B.H.Belle, scored heavily and rapidly; Yorkshire were scarcely able to score at all. What Essex did do and Yorkshire did not created the abiding impression of a match contained within a day and a morning.

More often, though, it is the part rather than the whole that stays in memory; the hour or the day that gleams more brightly than the match. This is natural enough, I suppose, because in cricket more than in most games the incident can be isolated and relished for intrinsic satisfaction. Some of the greatest innings ever played, some of the finest bowling ever accomplished, came as contribution to matches that need the scorebook to give them shape and identity.

Great cricketing achievement must, of course, be significant in context, influential on the course of the match as known at the time. The second-innings century of lively hitting on the last afternoon of an inevitably drawn game is not to be measured in the same terms as first-day batting with the match result unknown. Second-innings wickets taken against a background of ample time and runs to spare cannot compare with the bowling success that creates advantage.

Miller created advantage on the Melbourne morning when he opened the Test against England with nine overs in which he took three wickets for five runs. That Australia lost advantage and, indeed, lost the match, in no way reduces the splendour of Miller's performance. Hammond's 240 in the Lord's Test of 1938 retained all its magnificence though the match itself faded into a draw.

Those two occasions rank high in my long list of days remembered. I need a reference book to check mathematical detail, but I need no prompting of current account or spur of rival reminiscence to live the hours again.

The English summer of 1938 was neither a drought nor a deluge and the Test matches carried a fair representation of the weather pattern. At Trent Bridge, Lord's and The Oval the sky was more often clear than cloudy; at Headingley there was dampness, darkness and pervading atmosphere of *Wuthering Heights*; at Old Trafford not a ball was bowled.

The Lord's Test began on a sunny morning and therefore in the most impressive setting cricket can offer. A crowded Lord's in late June, with England meeting Australia, is a romance of living history, a touchstone of tradition, a feature in a way of life. Chariot races in the Colosseum were to Roman civilization as Test matches at Lord's are to the British. Perhaps the magic is fading a little with cricket's increasingly blatant commercialism, with the multiplication of 'occasions' that cannot justify their advertised appeal and, above all, with the revision of sporting and social custom. Gain from freedom to discard a shirt, to chant moronic praise or protest, to defy the ground rules made for general convenience must be set against loss of wonderment in the presence of the exceptional, elevation derived from grandeur.

In 1938 the character of Lord's was clear and commanding, like the bell that announced approaching play. It was a character that acknowledged, without apology, convention and privilege. Captains going from the pavilion to make formal inspection of the pitch and the toss for choice of innings went in flannels and blazer—not, as I have seen on another ground in recent times, in a cardigan and slippers. Rituals were known to players and spectators and observed by both, who thus dignified themselves in their sharing of ceremony.

When Bradman led Australia into the field the background for memorable cricket was ideal. In sunshine a crowd as big as the ground could hold covered stands and boundary edge with colour. No one at Lord's that morning could have failed to be without response to a sense of occasion.

Occasion sharpened the significance of routine. The five-minute bell and the appearance of the umpires brought an obedient settling of spectators in their places, with a belated scurry to vantage point visible here and there. The Australians flooded out to field, scattering as soon as they had escaped from the pavilion gate. Barnett and Hutton, walking briskly to open the England innings, were given acknowledgement, reflecting appreciation for their partnership of 219 in the

Trent Bridge Test. In cathedral hush McCormick began his run-up to deliver the first ball.

Within half an hour he had taken three wickets. We in the pews of the old Press Box alongside the pavilion whispered knowingly of 'green' in the pitch and the early-morning liveliness of Lord's as Hutton and Barnett were caught at short leg and Edrich, attempting a hook, played on.

At twenty for two Hammond came out to bat. In an Impressionist painting he would have trodden a red carpet down the pavilion steps and across the outfield on his way to the crease. In no possible way could royal progress have been more regal than in Hammond's walk to the wicket. It was made at normal pace, without the hurry of anxiety or the deliberation of tactical device. It focussed the attention of every man, woman and child in Lord's by the strength of its assurance and the beauty of its physical attributes.

Hammond's walk was the most handsome in all cricket, smooth in the evenness of stride, precise in balance. It was a flow of movement linking stillness to stillness. It was, as much as any feature of athletics, the poetry of motion.

Hammond came to the wicket through many different approaches. At Bristol he had awkward steps to negotiate from a first-floor dressing-room; at Headingley he had to press his way through spectators; at Gloucester among other places he would prise himself from a deck-chair. By repute he was not a compulsive watcher of cricket and there is record of his having to be nudged from sleep to take his innings and of his making apology for desertion of a card-school.

Wherever and however he appeared he was graceful and magnetic, but at Lord's in 1938 he epitomized himself. He adorned the picture by being so perfectly in keeping with it.

In his walk from pavilion to pitch he stirred the heart and dimmed the eye with pride for cricket in a magic moment. He came like a king and he looked like a king in his coming.

I am conscious of my tendency to invest the commonplace with a romanticism of my own making; I am inclined to colour with a 'Light that never was on sea or land' and I am not above suspicion of exaggerating virtues and overlooking flaws in consideration of cricket heroes and heroics. 'Heavens above,' I can hear the realist protest, 'what a song and dance to make about a batsman simply walking to the wicket.'

There is no defence against such complaint. Hammond was, in physical terms, doing no more and doing it no better than on hundreds of occasions. He always walked with grace and confidence and dignity, but this time there was an added quality as clear, to me, as though he had been wearing a purple cloak. It was the assurance of being the right person in the right place at the right time.

I was not alone in thinking so. Over the years innumerable people who were at Lord's that day have remarked on the impressiveness of Hammond's entry in the atmosphere of excitement created by the fall of wickets to McCormick's lively bowling.

Some of that impressiveness is no doubt a product of hindsight, a reflection of glory that followed. Had Hammond been leg-before for nought we should probably remember his walk out more readily than his walk in, but Hammond was not l.b.w. for nought and his entry did presage and perhaps contribute to one of the great innings of cricket.

On 30,000 watchers, sitting or standing, comfortable or crushed, the effect of Hammond at the crease was soothing. Facts insist that the alarms of the morning were not over, for England lost their third wicket at thirty-one, suggesting that McCormick could still extract lift and swing from the new ball. Hammond quelled the alarms by saying to Australia's bowlers and using deeds for words: 'Enough; this is a batting occasion.'

By lunch-time the character of the day had been established. Hammond had scored seventy and Paynter had stayed with him, virtually unremarked in the shadow of the Hammond splendour. There had been no assault born of passion on the bowling, no hitting in desperation, no grim defiance of a fearsome enemy. The whole glory of Hammond's batting was its easefulness. The force employed was made the more astonishing by its disguise under rhythm. Nobody troubled to chase the ball to boundary as Hammond directed it through the covers or between the bowler and mid-off, but Hammond's driving contained no element of brutality. Its power was in its artistry.

Afternoon and evening of this Hammond day were the morning's harmony repeated. Hammond scored seventy more runs between lunch and tea and another seventy before the close, when England were 409 for five wickets. Paynter shared a stand of 222 and came to notice mainly because of his dismissal, leg-before, for ninety-nine.

Paynter was rarely an anonymous batsman. He could drive and he could hook and he had frisky feet. In the afternoon he scored at the same pace as Hammond, rather in the manner of a boy allowed to enjoy his own Christmas present after the adults have played their fill. Paynter was in the match with admirable contribution; so was Ames; so was O'Reilly, bowling for Australia, but they were all background figures, emphasizing Hammond.

Forward strokes were the basis of Hammond's innings and the drive was its glory. In scoring 210 Hammond must surely have collected many on-side runs but they are registered in the scorebook, not in memory. The mind's eye captured and the heart treasured pictures of drives from the front foot, drives from the back foot scorching through the covers to be greeted with 'Oo-oh' and 'Aa-ah' of wonder before acknowledgement by crackle of clapping. The clapping applauded the effectiveness of the stroke, its product in runs; the spontaneous cries of wonderment were tribute to the magic in the stroke's creation. Such response is the accolade of the cricket spectator and is rarely given, because it is drawn from a quality of batting rarely presented.

The three seventies that made up Hammond's 210 not out

corresponded with the divisions of day. The first seventy was characterized by invigorating freshness of the morning; the afternoon seventy had a leisurely air, suggesting warmth in the sunshine; evening was calm. Not one of the 30,000 of us could have gone away from Lord's without a satisfaction, a roundness, a sense of the complete. 'Ripeness is all,' we echoed.

The Adelaide Oval has an easy and pleasant approach from the city's shopping and business area. The way lies across a wide bridge spanning the Torrens river and its embankment gardens and then along pathways through lawn and rosebeds to the main gates of the ground.

The bridge links city centre with residential suburbs and carries public transport, thus permitting an improbability to be raised on my behalf one sunny afternoon. At the kerbside on the bridge five or six strikingly attractive young ladies were standing beneath a sign that read: Queue for Kilburn. An envious companion assured me that the girls were merely waiting for a local bus.

The Oval itself is world-renowned for its setting and outlook, though, as at Worcester, the beauty depends on the viewpoint of the beholder. From the seats in the Adelaide stands the background to cricket is cathedral spire and distant blue hills, but from the open embankment of the popular side the eye that roves from the play finds little refreshment in severe outlines and garish paintwork.

One February morning in 1955 I gave myself the most uninspiring of all vantage points in the Oval. With my back to the main scoreboard and the cathedral I looked away from the soothing prospect of the hills down the length of the brown field towards the harsh colour and black shadows at the end of the semi-circling stand.

My asceticism on this fifth morning of the fourth Test was self-imposed. I went to this unfrequented part of the ground to watch the cricket in a quietness the Press Box or the crowded stand could not offer, to seek such freshness as still remained in the air of a scorching summer and, most of all I suppose, to relax in detachment. Touring cricketers, and to a lesser extent touring cricket-writers, need occasional recreation derived from wearing the face of personal joy or sorrow instead of the façade appropriate to professional proprieties.

The Test was in delicate balance after four days of careful manœuvring for advantage—or, more strictly, for avoidance of disadvantage. England, batting second, had led by eighteen runs on first innings and had taken three Australian second-innings wickets for sixty-nine when stumps were drawn on the fourth evening. That all these three wickets had been taken by Appleyard after Benaud and Johnson had been the principal bowlers for Australia suggested that spin bowling would direct the remaining course of the match on a pitch that never had lifted the heart of fast bowlers.

The fifth morning, by popular estimate, was to be conclusive. If England's spin bowlers, Appleyard and Wardle, could take immediate command England would be spared a daunting fourth innings. If that fourth innings demanded 200 runs or more Australia were probable winners of the match.

My expectations no doubt followed the general and logical pattern of opinion, but in my vigil near the sightscreen I isolated myself from prophet's boom and questioner's pleading. I wanted to avoid anticipation, analysis and argument; to watch in that state of consciousness without concern experienced in the first moments of recovery from anaesthesia.

In this 'willing suspension of disbelief' I had no need to wonder why England's opening overs were given to speed instead of the anticipated spin. I merely saw Statham bowling and I felt no reaction of astonishment or elation when McDonald, pushing forward like a man with sleep still on his eyelids, was clean bowled. At the time it never occurred to me that England were winning the match illogically; that Australian batsmen were being overwhelmed by Statham and Tyson when they should have been struggling against Appleyard and Wardle. The Australian collapse seemed natural enough on the simple premise that the bowling was superior to the batting, but I thought I had better make a little bow to cricketing superstition by remaining where I was to keep the spell of desired success unbroken. Australia were eighty-three for eight when I returned to the Press Box.

I stayed there after lunch and knew no moment of mental ease or physical comfort until the match had ended. The afternoon temperature was not exceptionally high, but Adelaide in February is always hot and sun and sensation made the Oval a cauldron of bubbling emotion. By now some legend will surely have grown of the 'man who slept through it', but such distinction would mark a sorrow, for this was a cricketing experience granted only once or twice in a lifetime.

The Adelaide Press Box is an enclosure in the stand, open to the sights and sounds expressing public opinion as well as generating its own atmosphere. The afternoon uncertainty was in vivid contrast to the morning assurance. I saw formality turned into the fiercest fight. I felt, with every other spectator, the approach of the impossible. I bolstered with reason and recall of history a faith tested close to its limits. Detachment was out of the question and hysteria was a communal threat.

England's need was no more than ninety-four runs. Time was of no consequence; weather and pitch required no consideration; Australia were a weakened bowling force because of Johnson's arm injury. By no extravagance of calculation could an Australian victory have been reasonably devised as Keith Miller bowled the first over.

By the end of it one wicket had fallen. By the end of his third over three wickets had fallen and England's total was twelve. Prophecy, prospect and probability were upsidedown.

It is a commonplace of sportswriting to say that some individual 'dominated the play' and the expression has lost its force, but it could have been properly used of Miller on this Adelaide afternoon. For an hour and more he commanded eyes, thoughts, hopes and fears. He rose gigantic in cricketing stature.

To the end of my cricket-remembering I shall know the agonies and ecstasies of that afternoon; feel the heat, shudder to the shouting as wickets fell, tremble with anticipation in the silences. Miller took us all beyond the contest between bowler and batsman, beyond the conventions and contrivances of a game, into the spiritual experience that is claimed as a consequence of art and a justification for it.

Miller himself would, I am sure, request dissociation from such elevated sentiment. He was not self-sacrificially defending Australia's last bridge,

> facing fearful odds
> For the ashes of his fathers
> And the temples of his gods.

Not he. He was bowling in the mood of the moment, taking cricket in its context of the day.

If I had spoken to him as I am now writing of him and of the emotions he inspired he would have said: 'Aw—come off it. I was only bowling.'

By only bowling he yorked Edrich and had Hutton and Cowdrey caught in the slips. By only bowling he compelled defence of desire by unconvincing logic; the philosophy that says 'It can't happen here. We must be able to raise ninety-four runs. Leg-byes, no-balls, edged boundaries, soon mount up. There is plenty of batting to come.'

Even as we sought the comfort of such self-assurances May played back to Miller and the ball climbed sharply from the pitch to the splice of the bat. May was surprised and Miller was surprised and though the bowler changed direction in his follow-through and made swift strides up the pitch he could not reach the falling ball. In cold analysis the catch never was the chance of a catch, but in a thousand bedazzled eyes it was a looming reality.

May and Compton, who were not by nature subservient

batsmen, challenged Miller only by inviting him to exhaust himself against their defensive shield. Through this partnership of repulse the scoreboard scarcely moved, but the tension scarcely slackened. The contest seemed to be entirely between Miller and the batsmen, with the overs from the other end somehow failing to impinge on the consciousness, but that impression is a measure of a major character rather than depreciation of the minors.

There was no assurance, no relaxation on the field and around it. Initiative remained with Miller until May and Compton played him into a rest from bowling. Miller tossed back his unruly hair, passed a forearm across the waterfall of his brow and moved casually into the covers for Johnston's bowling.

May drove, firmly but with fractional mistiming that lifted the ball, never more than waist-high, so that it would have pitched just short of extra-cover and, unchecked, would certainly have rattled against the boundary fence. A catch was a consideration only because Miller created one.

In three floating strides he reached the point of interception, swooped with hands outstretched at ankle height, plunged to earth under his own momentum, rolled over and claimed his prize. England were forty-nine for four and nobody believed that the match was merely awaiting collection by obvious winners.

Miller's catch raised controversy. As I remember, May moved immediately towards the dressing-room when Miller took the ball, but Compton checked him with a cry: 'Go back.' A possibility was presented that the ball had been lost and recovered during Miller's fall. I have no direct observation to offer because the fieldsman had his back to the Press seats and his body shielded my view of the ball, but I never questioned the catch in the instant of its making—merely marvelled. I suppose I felt then, as I am inclined to feel now, that whether or not the catch were genuine it ought to have been, like an anecdote revealing character.

Miller could not win the match for Australia, by bowling or fielding, but he made England's victory a convalescence of relief after fever of uncertainty, delight augmented after the gloom of doubt. His was the day, though he held the stage for only an hour of it, though his team went down to defeat, though in technical excellence and effective endeavour he was matched by England's morning bowling and England's final batting.

With a five-wicket margin of victory the match clearly reached a predictable end before its last overs, but it never descended to anti-climax. The winning hit was made by Evans, whose catchphrase through the tour had been 'We'll be there at the finish', and before the runs could be recorded arms were flung on high, cheers drowned the conventional clapping and more spectators were standing than sitting to applaud the players from the field.

7. *Weatherbound*

Cricketing days remembered are coloured by the weather. Sometimes it is a backcloth, sunshine to a century, heavy atmosphere to a bowling triumph, rain or threat of rain to a dramatic finish. Always it is a significant item.

No description of cricket is complete without indication of the weather conditions and the state of the pitch. Somewhere, somehow, the circumstances of play must be conveyed if the picture is to have life and meaning. Without a setting some flavour of the game is lost and some truth. A journalistic joke reflects wisdom when agency representatives are required to report at each day's beginning: 'Weather fine (dull) (showery) (cold). Wicket good (soft) (broken). Hours of play 11.30 to 6.30 or variations.'

I marvel that cricket writers can cross the world and report a match in Sydney that might have been taking place in Sussex for all the indication given. Time and place, light and shade, heat and cold are factors as relevant as the bowling figures or the sum of boundaries hit. The feel of a cricket occasion may be even more significant and memorable than the facts in the scorebook.

I shall always believe that weather changes scarcely mentioned in contemporary accounts were an England ally during the tour of 1954–5. The strong wind that raised Tyson's pace at Sydney has been well recorded but there is little mention of blessings England received at Melbourne and Adelaide.

The Melbourne Test covered a week-end of exceptional heat in which a north wind seared the city. Of the Sunday conditions I have two illustrative recollections. My hotel room had a window which could be opened top and bottom and which ran almost from floor to ceiling. For an hour in the morning I was writing at a desk by the window with the lower pane pushed up to allow breeze though not direct sunshine into the stifling room. I was wearing khaki shirt and shorts, but not the threequarter-length stockings that would have made the attire conventional for outdoor appearance in Australian midsummer. When I moved from the desk I felt my legs to be stiff and sore and examination showed them to be scorched as though they had been in a flame.

Later in the morning I sought to refresh myself with a bar of chocolate that had been in a drawer overnight. I would have needed a spoon to eat it.

Though the wind had dropped before Test-match play continued the temperature was in the nineties Fahrenheit at breakfast-time on the last morning, when England had to take eight wickets before Australia scored 165 more runs. The state of the deteriorating pitch suggested that chances were about even for batsmen and bowlers.

Before the start of play Denys Rowbotham, of the *Guardian*, and I were taking our customary mid-morning tea in a refreshment bar near the Press Box. The room was airless and sweltering so we moved outside with our drinks, preferring the burn of sun to the threat of suffocation. As we sipped and speculated we became conscious of a sharp change in the air. The sky stayed a brilliant blue, the sun lost none of its brightness and power, but breathing became easier, the skin felt fresher, alertness returned.

In this 'cool change', as Australians name it, temperatures can fall by as much as 20°F within an hour. In this case they fell from summer distress to summer delight and with fast bowling of sustained resolve Tyson and Statham tumbled Australia to defeat by 128 runs. The bowling and fielding were literally inspired.

At Adelaide in the same series a similar climatic benevolence was bestowed, though this time over a whole match. In the preceding week normal life in the city had been scarcely tolerable. Daytime temperatures soared beyond the 100 and the dark hours brought little relief; mosquitoes also could not sleep. Road-surfaces melted and policemen on traffic duty needed the protection of a sunshade. Bush-fire smoke crowned Adelaide's circling hills and the sand at Glenelg was too hot for beach recreation.

Test-match eve brought the change. Down dropped the temperature, up went the spirits. The game was played in hot weather, but not in a furnace, as it would have been a week earlier. England's players, fulfilling up-country engagements in cooler areas, escaped the Adelaide heat-wave—and they won the Test match.

The most spectacular climatic interference with cricket in my personal experience was undoubtedly the Brisbane thunderstorm of 1946. I have seen Lord's briefly carpeted in white by hailstones; I have seen Old Trafford submerged in half an hour; I have seen the lower part of Headingley flooded knee-deep, but I have never known anything comparable with the Brisbane visitation.

It began with an ominous calm, with a swift darkening of the tea-time sky. There was no rain as the players strolled from the field after appeal against the light. There was no rain with the first steely-blue flashes of lightning. This was a period of grace for seeking shelter, though the shelter had to be close at hand.

The first raindrops made splashes big enough to represent a little pool and whirlwinds spiralled litter ten and twenty feet in the air. Raindrops became hailstones, big enough and hard enough to bounce from the open seats and terracing. In the Press Box, which was at that time little more than improvised accommodation at the back of the main stand, we spoke to each other in wonder at the density of the downpour and the intensity of the lightning.

Five minutes later we had no means of verbal communication. Each one of us was cut off from all others in a cacophony that defied the loudest shout. Shrieking wind tossed tarpaulin from the pitch and flattened sightscreens. The downpour of hailstones stretched a curtain across the field and rattled on the roof as though all the kettledrums in the world were being played together. Anyone without some feeling of fear must also have been without imagination.

English weather is less alarming but it can bring memorable discomfort to cricketing occasions. May days can be cruelly cold. Derbyshire and Yorkshire once abandoned a match at Chesterfield in snow that was still lying over the whole field as the players left the ground on the way to their next engagement. Arthur Mitchell once fielded at Fenner's with two pairs of flannels over his pyjama trousers.

I think I touched my nadir of reporting discomfort on the Castle ground at Colchester. The whole day was damp and cold and windy and the Press accommodation was a small tent, sited to face the breeze. In late afternoon the rain came, driving before the wind into every corner of the tent. There was nowhere else to go; the pavilion was on the far side of the ground and the nearer stands were plank-and-scaffolding and unroofed.

A tide of water swept across the trestle writing-table and the grass beneath the freezing feet was liquid mud. There had been sufficient play before the rain to demand at least a half-column account and for some reason, presumably telegraphic, it had to be written at the ground. The desk was useless because paper became soaked and the words illegible as soon as they were written. I was cold; I was wet; I was miserable.

I took a chair to a corner of the tent, turned my back to the field and rain, gave the paper such protection as I could with raincoat and huddled body and used knees for a desk. The substance of the message, its character and its dispatch have long since passed from mind but I remember with gratitude the hotel service that provided a hot whisky to be taken, for medicinal purposes of course, in a hot bath. The next time I was in the *Yorkshire Post* office an innocent and well-meaning colleague asked if I were enjoying my 'summer holiday'.

8. Cup Final

I am not a committed advocate of one-day cricket for first-class cricketers. I believe that this popular fancy of the present time to be a contradiction of purpose and inevitably self-defeating in its object of attracting spectators to cricket. First-class cricketers, in my belief, need more than fifty or sixty overs or an hour or two in which to express themselves.

Cricketers of first-class quality need more scope than the one-day match can offer them. Without scope they cannot develop their potential or, having developed, they cannot maintain the standards of which they are capable. Cricketers who have attained first-class level by playing in first-class cricket—which is, of course, the only way to become first-class—will be the most successful one-day players; but should the one-day form become dominant the first-class player will not be developed and county cricket will not rise above club standards.

When one-day cricket for the counties was first proposed I was lukewarm towards it, fearful of long-term consequences of tradition. I saw in the Gillette Cup competition an attractive and useful variation in the summer programme, to be ranked in status with the Festivals or the old Gentlemen *v.* Players fixtures; I welcomed it as a parallel to the seven-a-side tournaments in Rugby Union football.

With the institution of the Gillette Cup I hoped for modifications in the county championship programme, but I believed then, as I believe now, that three-day cricket should preserve itself essentially through intrinsic attractions; that it should be first-class not only in name but in presentation. I was not living in the past when I deprecated the extension of one-day competitions and when I regretted attempted reform of the county championship by administrative detail of no basic significance. I was and am looking to cricket's future in my desire for first-class cricketers to play first-class cricket that can be understood and enjoyed by cricket followers.

I find the one-day form of cricket as offered by first-class cricketers unsatisfying mainly because of the inevitable artificial limitations imposed. One-day cricket is the appropriate cricket for most of us because it is the cricket of our capabilities and opportunity. Our techniques and temperaments will not sustain long innings or long bowling spells. Blessed with the advanced skills and disciplines we should want to move into a wider range and given the opportunity we invariably do. The illogicality is moving back again. First-class cricket is an extension and development by the gifted few of afternoon cricket attempted and enjoyed by the many, but the quality of the few has to be diminished or disguised in afternoon compression. One-day cricket cannot be a distillation of first-class essence; it must become either a restriction or a parody. The greater and more complicated the artificialities the more blatant the parody.

In apparent paradox one-day cricket has provided fewer days to remember than single days of truly first-class cricket. Few great innings have been played or can be played simply because circumstances do not permit them. Even in the occasional big score sustained mastery is not required because the bowling challenge automatically diminishes. It is a cricketing nonsense to suppose that five bowlers will all be equally testing on one afternoon. It is a cricketing contradiction of common sense that bowling authority established or close upon establishment should have to be relinquished because of overs limitation.

The longer one-day matches—or, more strictly, single-innings matches—do, of course, provide occasional hours of rare splendour, occasional achievements to catch the breath in anxiety and admiration. Lancashire contrived such an hour in their famous victory over Gloucestershire at Old Trafford, and Yorkshire made magic in the Gillette Cup Final with Surrey in 1965.

In both those instances the special quality of the day was influenced by the climatic conditions. Lancashire won when by normal assessment of light they could not see to win. Yorkshire won when all the probabilities were against any play at all.

Yorkshire travelled to London for their first Final in pouring Friday rain. The southward miles raised increasing resignation to at least one day's waiting at Lord's—and one idle day would have involved another because there was then no provision for Sunday play. Harder and harder the evening rain teemed down and arrival at King's Cross found London awash. Through the talk of a fully covered pitch and a new drainage system optimism was muted beneath continuing bedtime rainfall.

Saturday morning brought fair weather and an encouraging forecast but nobody went to Lord's with any anticipation of play before lunch or even of a start much before late afternoon. We were astonished. A first sight of the field presented almost as much sawdust as turf but the ground staff were inspiringly industrious and efficient and the start of the match was put back no more than an hour and a half.

This in itself was a joyful excitement. Players and others professionally involved make provision for the extension or postponement of a one-day match but there are thousands for whom rearrangement spells abandonment of direct participation. The decision to play, and so unexpectedly early, created its own atmosphere of eagerness on the Grandstand, on the Mound and in front of the Tavern.

Yorkshire won the toss and batted first, but their beginning was timid and tremulous. Taylor was clearly uncomfortable and Boycott was resolutely unadventurous. Time and, more significantly, overs passed without any establishment to the innings. Without a wicket falling the bowling looked better than the batting and Surrey looked like assuming command of the match.

Taylor's dismissal when his score was nine was not unexpected but it was, by the proof of events, unfortunate for Surrey. It brought Close to the crease in a revision of the published batting order. The Yorkshire needs of the moment were obvious enough and Close, never short of self-confidence, came to give a captain's inspiration by example instead of by exhortation.

He challenged the throttling bowling with speculative pull and square cut and he bustled the suffocating field-setting to a more respectful disposition. He breathed urgency into the batting by his approach and he stirred Boycott from inactivity. The run-rate was raised from below two an over in the first hour to an overall three an over by the end of the second. Bowling changes compulsory under rules of the match would in any case have been enforced by the batting. Surrey looked to be the struggling side.

The afternoon play carried Yorkshire to complete authority and great glory. Boycott took the popular fancy with his innings of 146, which mounted to thrilling domination, but the source of Yorkshire's batting inspiration was Close, who scored seventy-nine and directed the course of the decisive second-wicket partnership. Boycott's batting was technically flawless from the stern defence of its beginning to the wonderful show of mastery in its later stages; Close played some sketchy strokes and always seemed at risk, but he was the leader of the counter-attack. His was the flourish without which Yorkshire could not have burst from bondage. He turned the Yorkshire morning from gloom to gratification; Boycott brought untrammelled joy to the afternoon.

Once their hands had grasped the match Yorkshire never relaxed grip. Boycott's magnificent boundaries were followed by supererogatory addition from the carefree hit-or-miss batsmen. Lord's echoed a continuous roar of Yorkshire approbation and as the total grew to record levels identification of loyalty was plain on faces of assurance and resignation.

Surrey's only hour of optimism in the match was the first. Once the avalanche that descended on them was moving destruction could be seen as sure and overwhelming. Theoretically, no doubt, Yorkshire's total of 317 from sixty overs was within reach, but in practice the Surrey batting had no hope. September evenings bring an early twilight; with enormous capital resources bowling and fielding enterprise can afford to be speculative; the feeling of the meeting was essentially of 'when' rather than of 'whether or not'.

From my corner of the Press Box I watched the Surrey innings with a selfish eye. I wanted to be back in Scarborough on Sunday morning, not I must confess to attend the traditional Cricket Festival church service, but to play in the traditional Festival golf match at Ganton. My prospects as Surrey began batting ranged from the Gillette Cup Final extending into a second day to a train leaving King's Cross at 7.30, with an all-night journey and bleary-eyed golf as a possible alternative.

Edrich and Stewart discouraged my hopes of golf in a watchful opening partnership. They took the total to twenty-seven and indicated Surrey intentions of compelling Yorkshire to bowl sixty overs. I waved a metaphorical good-bye to the 7.30 from King's Cross and began to wonder about hotel accommodation for the week-end.

The total was twenty-seven when Trueman, bowling with the shadow of the pavilion behind him, dismissed Edrich, Smith and Barrington in the space of four balls.

Nobody, thereafter, contemplated match-extension, though the last-wicket batsmen were good-naturedly obstructive after Illingworth had helped himself to three wickets in one over. From near the Main Gate I saw the last wicket fall and, excusing myself from the presentation scenes and ceremony, I travelled north by the 7.30 to York. In one day I had seen the completion of a match that might well have failed to begin, that brought a record total and a record individual score; that ranged spectatorial responses from anxiety to delirium of joy or, alternatively, from anticipation to disappointment in a degree of disbelief; that, unwittingly, influenced a game of golf 250 miles away.

9. Parson's Play

One notable Vicar of Esholt in the West Riding of Yorkshire was undoubtedly a practitioner of Christianity as interpreted by the Church of England, and his primary calling was to service of his Master and parishioners; but he did like his cricket.

Sunday matches were beyond his reach but only the most pressing of counter-claims was likely to forbid him a mid-week indulgence within reasonable geographical range. He was not, though he might have been, the cleric involved in the story of the Dales farmer who sought from his vicar a mutually convenient time for burial of an aged relative. After various possibilities had been considered and rejected the farmer concluded:

'Tell thi what, Vicar; we'll up-end him in t' church porch and tha can side him when tha's time'—'side' being the vernacular for 'put away'.

The Reverend C.E.D.Crane had precisely the qualities to maintain, stabilize and glorify those loosely bound associations formed to bring cricketers together entirely for the purpose of cricket; clubs, usually of fanciful title, demanding the minimum and yet the maximum of qualification for membership. They ask not who you are or what you do, where you live or how you live, but would you like to play, with kindred spirits, for such satisfactions as the day might bring.

Parson Crane, as I knew him in the 1930s, found such satisfactions with the Craven Gentlemen C.C. The parish of Esholt never was in the Yorkshire district of Craven but, then, the club was people, not residences, and quickly spread beyond its area of origin. It had no clerical basis of membership and, by circumstantial evidence, was open to heathen or heretic. It played in no league or competition, found fixtures where it was welcomed and, in its capacity as host, borrowed or hired a ground.

Opponents were as varied as its own representation. The C.G. touched the fringes of first-class cricket in meetings with Sir Julien Cahn's XI and did battle on village greens with equal enthusiasm and delight. Schools were visited and 'home' matches at Ilkley and Harrogate gave welcome to such travelling sides as the Frogs from Kent and the Catamarans from London's coloured community. The C.G. played where and when they could arrange a game and rarely, in my recollection, attempted to turn out the same team twice. Selection was by call for volunteers and when the fixture list appeared in Spring there was eager thumbing of business diaries.

S.M.J.Woods, captaining Somerset on one occasion, is reputed to have surveyed the team-sheet presented to him and remarked: 'Well, I don't know him, or him, but I've heard of him—he's a helluva fine golfer.' C.G. captains-for-the-day were frequently left in the same confusion.

Unfamiliarity sometimes evoked misunderstanding. In one match approaching climax with a few runs wanted and only one wicket to fall I was supposed to be the batsman in charge, responsible for protecting a number eleven who had bowled well but had disclaimed any batting ambition or competence. On the last ball of an over I called for the tactical single and made my running in continuation of the stroke. From half-way down the pitch I saw my partner immobile and cupping a hand to his ear.

'I beg your pardon,' he was murmuring in the quiet tones characteristic of the deaf. 'What did you say?'

Parson Crane epitomized the purpose and character of the Craven Gentlemen of the 1930s. He would play whenever he could, in minor engagement or major. His enthusiasm was unquenchable and his authority in the captaincy invariably bestowed on him was benign. He wanted everybody, including himself, to do well in every match; he sought always 'a summer of roses and wine' and by exercise of imagination and reminiscence he could contrive high holiday from a wet day.

I never knew him offer a harsh or a hasty word and, heaven knows, there was scope for both in some of the C.G. techniques. Seen through Crane's spectacles all cricket was sweetness and light and the failures of today were considered only as balancing factors for successes in prospect tomorrow. Parson Crane was at this time about sixty years old.

White hair wisped from beneath his multi-coloured cap and his tackle preserved a flavour of bygone custom. His bat was dark with oil and age and tenderly bandaged. His pads were short and narrow and ventilated, as Ranjitsinhji had favoured, and 'Ranji' represented Crane's pride and sorrow mingled. 'I think I might have got a Blue,' he told us, without a trace of arrogance, 'but Ranji came up at that time.'

On the field Parson Crane's benevolent captaincy sometimes extended to the opposing side. Once when C.G. had lost the toss to St Peter's School, York, Crane led out his team saying to the accredited bowlers, 'I think I had better have a few overs myself to start with. We don't want to press the boys too hard.'

The sky was cloudless, the pitch perfection, and one of the incoming batsmen was named N.W.D.Yardley. I believe we struggled to an undignified draw after the School declaration.

In my recollection Crane's personal batting was orthodox in method, optimistic in approach and self-mystifying in effect. In match after match he played forward by the textbook and, pondering in the pavilion, he would muse: 'I can't understand how I was bowled; I was sure I played straight.' The technique had stayed with him but the years had taken toll of his timing.

Parson Crane appreciated cricket in terms of Sarah Battle's 'rigour of the game', but he also recognized social obligations implicit in playing host or visitor. He wanted to win, but certainly not at any cost. Gamesmanship, had he been able to understand it, in his team would have hurt him more than an epidemic of dropped catches. His was happy though sometimes haphazard cricket.

One mid-week afternoon of August he took a team to play against the staff and resident patients of a private hospital in Wharfedale. The playing area was a lovely sweep of lawn that fronted the mansion. Circling the boundary were trees, shrubbery and flower beds and behind long-on was a wooden summerhouse, furnished with a table and wicker chairs. The weather was sunny and exceptionally warm.

Before the contented captain led his team out to field he suggested that, in view of the heat and the general intention of the occasion, bowling strategy should be based on division of labour. 'We'll bowl two or three overs in turn,' he said, 'and spread out the field a bit.' The plan was accepted with unanimous approval.

After the first changes of bowling in the agreed routine our captain betook himself to the long field where he initiated conversation with the hospital superintendent, who was strolling at the boundary edge. The bowler of the moment, having completed his third over, looked towards the distant leader for relief and further instruction. No sign being returned, the bowler delivered a fourth over, and in the absence of any signal, a fifth. By this time a few wickets had fallen and the master-plan was in confusion.

More careful observation indicated the absence of the C.G. captain from his last-known fielding position. Calculation proclaimed him absent from the field altogether. At the fall of another wicket search exposed Parson Crane and the hospital superintendent sharing discussion and long, cooling drinks in the shade of the summerhouse. 'The game,' said the unrepentant captain, 'seemed to be going on all right.'

The game was, indeed, on the turn. A tottering innings was cemented by a confident and beautiful batting display that developed undisturbed through bowling changes both formal and of urgent necessity.

The batsman would have been remarkable without his performance. He was small, middle-aged and detached in manner. He was immaculately dressed in well-fitting flannels that looked brand-new; pads and boots were dazzling in the sunshine. The incongruity was a pair of obviously much-used and gaudy-coloured braces.

Cricket for the Craven Gentlemen took me to Stanford Hall, the home of Sir Julien Cahn. He had two private grounds, one at West Bridgford near Trent Bridge, but there a city bye-law of the period prevented Sunday play, so his team's two-day week-end fixtures were on his immaculate lawn where marquees served as dressing-rooms and refreshment accommodation.

Cahn's cricket was a self-indulgence of world-wide expression. He collected a team of international calibre and international mixture, challenged counties and clubs throughout the summer weeks and toured overseas almost every winter. He established a business organization of cricket to promote his obsessive hobby and his hospitality was lavish to a degree of embarrassment.

My own exploitation was unintentional and not on the field or at the dining-table. The visiting C.G. were being accommodated over the week-end at a Nottingham hotel and after the Saturday play we stayed at Stanford Hall for dinner. The later evening was devoted to bridge, a pastime for which I have no great aptitude and no extravagant enthusiasm, and I was happy in an arrangement that allowed me to leave the card-room for the library where I browsed alone through a famous collection of cricket books.

I browsed too long, beyond the acceptable time for a guest's departure and when I emerged from the library the card-school had long dispersed. Sir Julien accepted apology as compliment. He was, he said, delighted that his library should have proved so absorbing.

10. Patronage

From the little I saw of him on the field I could not rate Sir Julien Cahn highly skilled in the practice of cricket. Even under delicate disguises of compassion and contrivance he looked out of his class in his own teams.

His function and service came in the form of patronage. He had a dedication, an obsession, that would not be denied and need not be forsworn. The proportions of self-indulgence and altruism are beyond determination, but it would be both difficult and unkind to deny that Cahn's incursions brought more benefit than disadvantage to cricket. His interest and resources increased the sum total of cricket played; his grounds and teams created cricketing employment; his fixtures, in England and overseas, initiated cricket pleasure.

Patronage in one form or another has been of incalculable help to cricket. It translated the early game from a rustic pastime to a social concern, promoted it from the meadow to urban settings. Patronage established and extended a market for professional services. Patronage has kept clubs and county organizations from disbandment.

Personal patronage implies either a direct interest or a sense of social obligation. Some patrons gave their support because they liked to play or to watch cricket; some were merely acknowledging a conventional responsibility of community leaders. In either case cricket itself was not expected or required to sacrifice any fundamental independence of outlook. Those who played or watched accepted and enjoyed the current practices of the game. They wanted to share its established pleasures. Those who gave no more than the annual cheque had no wish to involve themselves in cricket.

Patronage on another basis came early into cricket when a

commercial purpose initiated development. The first English team to tour Australia made their journey and demonstrated their skills under sponsorship by the catering firm of Spiers and Pond, whose primary concern was not the welfare of cricket but advertising for the business of Spiers and Pond in Australia. Stephenson's cricketers were not even their sponsor's first choice as publicity material; they were substitutes for a lecture tour by Charles Dickens.

In the period of first-class cricket's expansion to public popularity and prosperity the private patron overshadowed the commercial sponsor. Cricket did not need to sell itself to advertising and its commercial significance was almost entirely concerned with individual endorsement of goods for sale. Nearly all these goods were in the form of cricketing equipment though as far back as the Golden Age there was a vendor's cry of 'George Hirst's toffee—and it is so nice' to be heard on Yorkshire grounds. Having known George Hirst, I suspect the use of his name earned him more in friendship than in financial return.

In the 1930s Hutton found a queue of suppliants outside his bedroom door the morning after he had completed his innings of 364, and when exploitation began to fall into the hands of agents Compton appeared on the hoardings in advocacy of the well-groomed man.

The first intrusions of commercial sponsorship were tentative and delicate. Clothing firms presented outfits to touring teams. Transport was provided. Business interests moved into cricket from the boundary edges. They flooded into the pavilion as soon as the door was left ajar.

Infiltration was logical enough in the context of the times. First-class cricket could not support itself in the manner of life to which it had been accustomed. The players, presenting themselves unattractively in an outmoded framework, failed to maintain public support, measured in attendances and gate-money. As many people as ever talked cricket, read cricket, wanted cricket, but they were not prepared to watch or to pay for a share without substance and flavour, which was what they were being offered in many county and Test-match occasions.

Without a rising income to balance rising costs first-class cricket had no prospect of survival. It had capital funds of tradition, techniques and public prestige, but they were stagnant or dwindling assets and they were clearly not producing adequate returns. In terms of City finance cricket was ripe for the take-over bid.

It came from commercial sponsors. They were prepared to buy shares in cricket, with, of course, the hope and intention of producing profits. The commercial sponsors who began to cultivate cricket in the 1950s and 1960s were not philanthropists; they saw cricket as an economical item in their advertising budgets.

The investment was unquestionably defensible in financial law and practice and in the moral outlook of commerce. A brand-name could be presented in association with cricket as justifiably as in a printed promotion or a television temptation. There was, indeed, a claim to social righteousness in providing cricket with an umbrella as protection against rainy days and cricketers with handsome prizes and perquisites.

An inevitable corollary of commercial sponsorship was the infusion of commercial enterprise. Advertising makes little impact with a light hidden under a bushel and the advertising departments spending money through cricket wanted the prestige they were paying for to be illuminated in eye-catching colour. The respectability attached to cricket in the public mind had to be capitalized in scrip issues of vivid presentation. Cricket and first-class cricketers were put on show in packaging of tinsel.

Some of the experiments failed. Single-wicket competitions, contests in throwing the cricket ball were quickly abandoned. The popular package proved to be the one-day or single-innings match. Sponsorship swiftly and properly, from its own point of view, concentrated on this novelty. It made good business. One sponsor pursued another in the promotion of single-innings competitions.

The rolling band-wagon necessitated revision of the pattern in cricket's traffic flow. To accommodate the new forms of the game the old county championship and touring programmes had to be adjusted and shortened.

Even the die-hard traditionalists appreciated the need for a stimulus to first-class cricket. The quality of play at both championship and Test level was clearly deteriorating and various experiments with the laws of the game and playing conditions added more confusion than interest. The traditionalist argument was that medication was being applied to the wrong ailment; championship cricket, not one-day artificialities, needed promotion, stimulus and sponsorship.

The new approach was, no doubt, honestly and honourably designed to support first-class cricket, but commercial interest inevitably overshadowed cricketing concern. Introduction of one novelty into the county programme was a blessing; the upheaval necessitated by two or three became an embarrassment.

Multiplication was also self-defeating. The established championship and a contrasting knock-out cup could be sustained happily in harness, without loss of significance for either, but an attempt to accommodate three or four competitions inevitably obscured some and weakened all. The commercial sponsors, naturally enough, beat their drums to secure instant, if superficial, attention. They were looking for dramatic ways of presenting an entertainment and concerned with the name of cricket rather than the game of cricket. Ironically they sponsored the reputation and talents of first-class cricketers to serve purposes outside first-class cricket.

Herein lies a basic difference between the older patronage and the recent sponsorship. Patrons seek to support and extend an art for its own sake and satisfactions. Commercial sponsors redirect the art and artists towards extraneous ends.

There is no right or wrong in the differing philosophies. A patron subsidizing musicians, painters, poets or cricketers is a benefactor to the arts. A sponsor commissioning art to be associated with a commercial product need be no less morally and socially acceptable. New sponsor is but old patron written in terms of changed economics.

Misgiving enters when art and artist suffer constriction and confinement. Commission me to paint a picture to the best of my ability and inspiration and you encourage art. Subsequent application of the picture to a soap advertisement is no denigration of the painting or the painter. But if you insist before I begin that my picture be so many inches square and contain only such-and-such colours then art's freedom of expression is threatened and my painting development is inhibited. Accepting such instruction I should sacrifice my artistic independence, which is, paradoxically, the quality that attracted you to me in the first place.

Both cricket and its commercial sponsors should, in my belief, take pains to ensure the independence of cricket as an art-form. Cricket, obviously, wants to be self-governing and self-propagating; to be in command of its own reforms, developments and ideals. Cricket's overriding interest is the welfare of cricketers.

Logically, cricket's preservation in autonomy is also the concern of sponsors, both ostensibly and in the secret places of the balance sheet. Cricket is useful for advertising only if it carries public favour and repute. Cock-fighting and bear-baiting would not now be considered desirable associations for advertising. Cricket's value to commercial sponsors is the established position of first-class cricket and first-class cricketers.

Without that established position available to them the sponsors, I feel, might turn away from cricket. If the game ceased to be displayed by cricket writing and television I wonder how long would be the queue of would-be sponsors. If the one-day forms of cricket ceased to be presented by players of first-class status I wonder for how long those forms would maintain a public appeal that attracts sponsorship.

Over-presentation of an advertising feature defeats its own object and because commercial sponsors are motivated by mixed incentive, with their own promotion necessarily dominant, cricket could suddenly find itself unwanted through changes in fashion or changes in taxation law.

The ultimate prosperity of first-class cricket must be based on the merits of first-class cricket. Living on subsidized 'instant' cricket to the neglect of first-class aims and standards is like feasting on windfalls from a neighbour's garden without troubling to cultivate your own apple trees. Some day the other orchard might fail to provide fruit. When the sponsors cease from sponsoring their present fancies, as they undoubtedly will because the fancies are little more than self-consuming novelty, cricket will be compelled to rebuild its first-class range to preserve existence and to fulfil a need of cricketers.

Forethought now, in cricket and in the current sponsorship, would open curtains to a sunlit future. Without scope, encouragement and assurance for first-class cricketers there is no future for cricket as a public entertainment and benefit and no future for commercial sponsorship.

11. *Fame in the Field*

Of cricket's basic divisions batting has always received the greatest acclaim and, rather illogically and certainly unjustly, fielding comes before bowling in popular fancy. Perhaps bowling needs a bowler's understanding for full appreciation and a closer proximity than ringside spectators can command. Cricket's supreme delights do, of course, include the sight of stumps scattered, of batsmen manifestly defeated even if not dismissed, of traps carefully laid and eventually closed, but on the whole you need to be where a spectator cannot be to relish the full savour of bowling effort and achievement. Bowlers tend to become cricketing heroes for what they do as distinct from how they do it. Woolley seen only once in an innings of thirty would be more likely to leave an indelible impression of greatness than, say, Bedser taking one for twenty in a spell of ten overs.

Exceptional fielding is easier to recognize. The diving slip catch, the swooping pick-up in the covers, the swift and accurate throw from the boundary edge make dramatic moments and memorable pictures in cricket. They are also within our understanding in the sense of being within our imagined compass. In our heart of hearts we know that the assured centuries of a Hobbs or a Bradman are beyond us; we imitate without really hoping to emulate the great bowlers. We can, however, see ourselves achieving an astonishing catch or throwing out some unwary batsman. We still believe in our fielding accomplishment long after experience has compelled recognition of our batting and bowling limitations.

Through this identification with our betters we are both touched to acclaim for fielding brilliance and inclined to harsh criticism of error in our observation of first-class cricket. All first-class cricketers, we feel, should be good in the field; most should be excellent and a few will be superlative.

The superlative have given delight in the highest range of cricket's pleasures. Fine fielding has always attracted appreciation and some players have earned a place in history as much by their fielding as by batting or bowling. A mention of E.M.Grace would recall his exploits, to say nothing of his impudence, at point.

In the early period of cricket the widest scope for fielding bravery and skill was offered to the bowler himself and to the long-stop, but when ground preparation became more sophisticated talent expanded at cover-point, in the long field and at mid-off. Vernon Royle and G.L.Jessop won fame in the covers. J.T.Tyldesley and David Denton challenged for supremacy at long-off and deep third man. George Hirst made himself a Rock of Gibraltar at mid-off. Australia matched England in team-fielding and man for man in specialization.

The Australians of 1921 drew almost as much admiration and respect for their fielding as for the authority in their bowling and batting. Their shining lights were J.M.Taylor and C.E.Pellew in the outfield, T.J.E.Andrews at cover or silly-mid-off and J.M.Gregory in the slips. Pellew was swift and graceful as a gazelle across the grass and his throw was hard and accurate with the conventional action of hand above the shoulder. Andrews, small and agile, took the balance and neat footwork of his batting into his patrol of the covers, but his most menacing aspect was the crouch beneath a big green cap a few yards in front of the batsman. His presence was a challenge and often enough his enclosing hands were a triumph.

For my youthful watching Gregory was a greater fielding fascination out of the slips than in his customary business position. He was an entertainment as he walked back to his bowling mark. He welcomed an apparent collusion by which the ball was thrown to him at awkward angles, sometimes high above him, sometimes to his boot-tops. Gregory, who was more than six feet tall, bent himself, stretched himself, contorted himself to make the most improbable catches with one hand or two, assuming a laugh-raising nonchalance as he continued his walk.

No doubt I am over-emphasizing in distant recollection. Gregory presumably chose his occasions for acrobatic indulgence and I do not claim to have seen it in a Test match; but I shall always associate the inconsequential catching with Gregory's cricketing character, as I associate the flick of the rolling ball from foot to hand with Cecil Parkin, who may not have been the originator of the trick but was the first regular exponent of it within my experience.

No fielding has made greater impact on my imagination and admiration than that of A.P.F.Chapman. I watched him with awe in his later playing years when he had become bulky and had transferred his artistry and courage to the close-in positions. He held wonderful catches in the gully and at silly-mid-off or silly-mid-on and his mere presence in those stations was an inhibition to batsmen, but in my most cherished recollection he remains a Cambridge University undergraduate patrolling the covers.

So, in the early 1920s, he won the heart of Scarborough Festival crowds. In those years he possessed all the heroic attributes. He was young, he was eager, he was talented.

He was tall and slim, he was fresh-complexioned and his hair was fair and curly. He was unmistakable in appearance and incomparable in activity. By repute and in effect he was not superior to Hobbs or one or two other cover-points of the time, but he was more readily identified with glamour. Hobbs could be an inconspicuous cover-point for hours on end, quietly efficient until the moment came for the darting pick-up and unerring throw that laid full charge on a batting misjudgement. Hobbs in his greatness saved runs by merely being at cover-point. 'Attempt nothing,' said his fielding attitude, 'and you will not be harassed.'

Chapman in the covers made a direct and spectacular challenge. 'Drive the ball past me if you can,' he proposed. 'Race my return.' At Scarborough, certainly, the challenge was manifest and magnificent. How many half-volleys outside the off-stump were deliberately offered in the Festival there is no knowing, but batsmen were happy to hit them as hard as they could in the general direction of Chapman and Chapman was happy to stand his ground, sprint to cut off the boundaries, pick up with one hand or two and throw in with thrilling speed. He was additionally threatening to the unwary because he was left-handed.

Chapman gave superb illustration of the below-the-shoulder throw that was characteristic of cover-point fielding in his time. This 'flick', acquired easily enough by practice, seems to have lost favour in recent cricket, though from thirty or forty yards it gives a quicker return than the bent-elbow, above-the-shoulder throw and offers a lovely, smooth flow of motion as a continuation of the running pick-up. Recent cricket, unhappily, has given decreasing scope for fielding distinction in the covers and the hard-hit off-drive swooped upon and swiftly returned is now a delight of play only rarely experienced. It created some memorable moments when the undergraduate Chapman was a darling of the Festivals.

Different aims and skills in fielding have developed with changing patterns of play. Inswing and inslant have demanded high expertise in the leg trap, which is now the region of the spectacular as was once the gully and the slips. Long before the era of inswing J.W.Hitch of Surrey won renown at short leg, but a whole host of fieldsmen are now picking up routine catches from genuine leg-glances or deflections from the inside edge of the bat. In this feature, at least, and in leg-side wicketkeeping, today's cricket need fear no comparisons.

The career of Tony Lock was full of bowling drama, ranging from triumph to disillusion, but whatever queries might be raised against his bowling technique no doubt whatever could be expressed over the brilliance of his fielding. Some of his catching at backward short leg defeated all eyesight except his own—and there was occasional suspicion that he must have been equipped with radar. Surely no human reactions could have enabled him to put grasping hands so swiftly and so precisely in the right place. The old vernacular term of 'blinder' could truthfully be applied to many of Lock's fielding feats.

Though his fame will stand for ever as a leg trap specialist Lock was a brilliant all-round fielder. He stopped Headingley's breath with a pick-up in the covers during a Test match against West Indies and he dived to catches from his own bowling that were not contemplated as catches until they were accomplished fact.

If my life depended on bowling success with assistance limited to only one fieldsman I think I should have asked for Lock before all others of his period. The choice would have required long pondering, for Lock played among great contemporaries. Neil Harvey, the Australian, must have been high-ranking in consideration. He was less of a specialist than Lock, spending much of his time in the covers and in the outfield where his fleetness of foot and his baseball throwing power could serve to best advantage, but he never looked out of place in the slips or in the gully. Wherever he was stationed, there lay fielding artistry.

Colin Bland, of Rhodesia and South Africa, would have been another strong candidate. He was, at international level, a batsman better than average but he drew spectators through the gates by fielding repute alone. His outstanding quality was athleticism rather than technique in specialization and his customary employment was in the midfield range on either side of the wicket. He was so agile in movement, so swift in anticipation, so sure in handling and so accurate in throw that he could safely be counted as a man and a half by his own side and was wisely counted as two men by his opponents. He stamped his authority on a Test-match day at Lord's in 1965 and he had the rare distinction of being commissioned to give one-man fielding demonstrations.

Bland played in twenty-one Test matches between 1961 and 1966 and might well have played in more had South Africa been able to stay in international cricket. His Test average was almost fifty and he made centuries against both England and Australia, so his fielding was clearly a bonus to his batting ability. He was not selected primarily because of fielding value.

Very few players ever have been so selected at county or Test-match level, but there have surely been instances of fielding ability, or lack of it, tipping the scales of favour. When P.J.Sharpe, of Yorkshire, was first chosen for England he was in poor form with the bat and his inclusion at Edgbaston against West Indies would have been difficult to justify had England not manifestly needed reliable slip fieldsmen. Ironically in the match itself Sharpe earned no fielding distinction but batted sturdily.

As a slip fieldsman he broke county records and in his best years was recognized as without peer in his particular position. He was not helped by the trend of cricket in his time and his proportion of catches held to chances offered must have been remarkably high to give the figures against his name.

There was a Yorkshire cricketer of brief career who said, on receiving congratulation over a catch, 'Sitha,' spreading his hands, 'when I get these on 'em they stick.' Sharpe would never have dreamed of such assertion on his own behalf, but he could have made it with a strong backing of fact. He held the ball with astonishing certainty whenever it came within grasp.

His reputation was built rather slowly. Shrewd Yorkshiremen were noting his achievements a season or two before they impressed themselves on general opinion. Before he became recognized as outstanding in the field he was languishing in ranks of batsmen who did not seem to be fulfilling early promise. He was one cricketer among many, meeting minimum requirements rather than rising to distinction.

Then the quality of his catching began to impinge on general consciousness. One brilliant catch followed another and a failure rather than a sucess became noteworthy. High, low, with right hand, left hand, both hands the offerings were gathered in with such assurance and consistency that in current nomenclature 'slips' became 'Sharpes'. Sharpe, like Bosanquet, created a cricketers' word.

Native skill and experience formed the basis for Sharpe's success in the slips. To make him outstanding he added an ingredient of high self-confidence. What he thought, or felt, he could catch he expected to hold and in large measure did hold. His reach was not that of the tall Tunnicliffe or Gregory, his mobility was not the flow of Hammond, but he had, by gift or acquisition, the sense of timing that marks the great. He was rarely seen to snatch at the ball; he let it come to him for his choice of intercepting moment.

Some of his most breathtaking catches gave an impression that the intercepting moment had been allowed to pass altogether. The ball seemed to be behind him, and probably was, when he took it. Like all accomplished slip fielders Sharpe put a trust in one hand where the use of two would have been a constriction and though by initial positioning he gave precedence to the right hand the left generally knew what to do on demand. As a batsman Sharpe might fairly be considered to have been slightly out of his class in the highest company; as a slip fieldsman nobody would deny him supreme ranking.

Another Yorkshireman, J.V.Wilson, appeared in a whole Test series entirely on a fielding qualification. He was a rather surprising choice for Hutton's tour of Australia in 1954–5 and his batting was proved inadequate, but he was made

D. B. Close – captain of Yorkshire, captain of England, captain of Somerset.

G. S. Sobers – batsman and bowler; the West Indian without a superior in all-round ability.

B. L. D'Oliveira – South African who made his cricket career in England.

twelfth man for every Test because there was no better all-round fieldsman in the side.

Wilson was not so much brilliant in a specialist position as thoroughly competent anywhere. He did build a high reputation at short leg but he went there mainly because that was the area of his greatest usefulness to the Yorkshire teams of his time. Had the catches been going to the long field or the covers or mid-wicket Wilson would have taken them as reliably as he did behind the batsman's back. He was the ideal substitute fieldsman because there was no position he could not fill.

Coloured cricketers have contributed greatly to glories in the field. Ranjitsinhji wove spells in the slips, or more usually in the gully, as well as at the crease. The quickness of his hand was prestidigitatory and with a turn of his head he would lead all eyes towards the boundary in search of a ball that was already in his pocket after a dazzling one-handed catch. Bewildered batsmen thought he had a perverted sense of humour.

West Indians brought a passionate energy to fielding, exciting to watch and almost as exhausting in observation as in the activity itself. Their early teams were full of fast bowling, eager batting and spectacular adventure in the field. L.N.Constantine, who became Sir Learie and a life peer, epitomized West Indian cricket in its young manhood. He was fast bowler, extravagant hitter and startling fieldsman. In the later cricketing sophistication of West Indies there were more potent fast bowlers, more disciplined and therefore more effective batsmen, but no greater fieldsman has yet appeared—and mere mention of Sobers and Lloyd is enough to measure the standard of competition.

Constantine was a truly wonderful fieldsman in that his fielding did arouse wonder. You did not say of his achievement 'That is excellent', 'That is brilliant', 'That is perfection'. You said, if you could speak at all, 'Oooh'.

He was the host in himself of overworked metaphor. He

wanted to field all the time, everywhere, and there were many moments when he appeared to be doing just that. There is no record of his having held a slip catch from his own bowling, but under his spell the impossible was not beyond imagined possibility. Certainly, he claimed 'caught and bowled' behind square leg and there were thousands of witnesses to confirm that from his bowling follow-through he picked up at short cover, threw down the striker's wicket, leapt to the rebounding ball near mid-on, turned and threw down the other wicket.

As memories become transformed into legends Constantine's fielding feats will no doubt be regarded with quizzical eyebrow and the polite scepticism accorded to fantasy. Such reaction would be misplaced. Constantine really was a fantastic fieldsman.

12. Cricket's Conduct

Between the wars, from 1919 to 1939 that is, first-class cricket changed in detail rather than in principles. The experiment of two-day county matches was no sooner tried than it was abandoned and the pattern of the seasons thereafter remained virtually undisturbed. The substance of summer's play was in the championship, with variety provided by such traditional interpolations as Gentlemen v. Players, a Test Trial and the end-of-season Festivals. Cream cakes were represented by Test matches for national consumption and engagements with the touring side for local feasting. Only Australia, coming to England at four-year intervals, and South Africa, visiting less frequently, were accorded the status of five-match Test series.

Throughout the whole period the course of cricket seemed to require no fundamental revision. The public appeal of the game remained constant, its prestige stayed high and continuity of high-quality recruits was preserved. To follow Sutcliffe, Hendren, Tate, with Hobbs and Woolley in autumn glory, came Hammond, Larwood, Verity and at the interruption which proved to be a watershed the young Hutton and the young Compton were taking up the torch of splendour in tradition. First-class cricket was certainly not falling in quality when Hitler's hordes began to ravage Europe.

There was, of course, contemporary criticism and there were changes in outlook and technique. Essentially, however, the game expanded from a fixed centre. The conduct, the intentions, the ideals of cricket were not in question as bowling strategy and legislation sought counters to the challenge of pitch-preparation, as pastime veered towards professional entertainment accepting a public responsibility.

Inter-war cricket was not all sweetness and light. It included bodyline, it included sharp disagreement between Middlesex and Yorkshire, between Nottinghamshire and Lancashire, between Sussex and Nottinghamshire and it included controversy deriving from the spoken word of Lord Hawke and the written word of Cecil Parkin and E.R.Wilson. In the peace interregnum cricket was not entirely peaceful.

Yet conflict, even at the most acute stage, was not revolutionary. The disputes were not over standards but over interpretations of ideals and principles held commonly by the disputants.

England and Australia both thought the well-being of cricket a fundamental consideration and in that belief they first argued and then settled the bodyline problems. Nobody wanted to change the underlying purpose of cricket, the meaning of the game enshrined in a conception implied by the negative 'It isn't cricket'. In the county quarrels the point was not so much a difference between right and wrong as whether or not certain behaviours were within the bounds of agreed right.

In cricket—and, for that matter, in all sport—there was a 'right thing'. It was not always done by individuals or representative bodies, but it was known and it was the yardstick for reference.

The immutable measure has been challenged in present-day philosophies of cricket, which, of course, respond to current social, political and economic philosophies. The very definition of 'right' has been brought into question. 'It isn't cricket' has tended to become 'That is cricket' within a revised morality.

In a transformation of outlook on acceptability there can be no precise moment of change. The undesirable of yesterday does not become the permissible of today between dusk and daybreak or at a stroke of the pen. Influences are cumulative and their pressures are frequently unappreciated until they have become effective.

That acceptabilities have changed is beyond argument and can be illustrated from almost any form of sport. In tennis it is now so commonplace to make public questioning of decisions by umpires and line-judges that such incidents pass without remark. In Association football the deliberate foul to save an impending goal receives positive commendation. In Rugby football an international coach has advocated superior cheating to overcome cheating. Athletes make no secret of drug-taking. These practices and equivalents in cricket have passed through phases of being overlooked, excused, anticipated and approved.

The behaviours of cricket in the mid-twenteith century have been more revolutionary than the revisions of cricket presentation and techniques. What once would have been regarded as taking or seeking a mean advantage has been reinterpreted as justifiable service in a cause. Deliberate waste of time is technical expertise. Exhibitions of lost temper illustrate dedication. Dressing-room privacies are legitimate material for profitable revelation. Self-concerns come before loyalties—for the player to the team, for the team to the club, for the club or organization to the game.

Attitudes on the field are reflected in attitude round the field and in commentary. Where means are claimed to justify ends and the essential end is winning, not for victory's own sake but for rewards of cash and aggrandizement, means come to be seen in pragmatic context.

Acceptance of deliberate obstruction and harassment on the field inevitably gives rise to jeering outbursts from spectators, designed to upset playing concentration. The competence of referees and umpires publicly questioned by players becomes rejection of authority from the terraces. Platforms for the controversial are increasingly available. 'Why not?' tends to be recognized as a standard of judgement.

Why should footballers not crowd round a referee in protest against a decision with which they disagree? At best they might secure a reversal of the decision; at worst they will gain the sympathy of committed followers and managerial support. Why should cricketers not throw down a bat or a ball to express amazement and discontent? Why should tennis-players not appeal to high heaven against fancied injustice?

To be sure, an older conception of sport would be harmed by such attitude in innumerable extension from the trivial to the basic, but the revolution is constructing a new conception. Yesterday's what 'isn't done' can be and manifestly is being abandoned. Whether or not the abandonment will prove to be for good or ill depends on viewpoint.

One outlook sees sport as a satisfaction of particular artistic talents, with social significance in the promotion of health, community interest and recreational benefit; as a controlled channelling of energy, ambition and the competitive urge. This sport is an education in physical development, in self-control of temperament, in appreciation of responsibility. This sport is a classroom accommodating pupils and teachers.

At first-class level this sport is tutorial by precept and example and it is promotional in its research into techniques. First-class cricketers attract a following by their entertainment, inspire by their demonstration and initiate development by their experiments. They are the graduates of the game.

It is their privilege and responsibility to set standards in 'pure' science, in 'art for art's sake', in satisfactions that are self-sufficing. Their aim is to practise cricket to the limits of its known range and then to seek expansion of the range—to the advantage of cricket. Derivative benefits of pleasant living, fame, prestige and social consequence are supplementary to the essential cause.

Thus academically conceived the first-class element in cricket assumes a morality of service. The question posed in every contemplated action becomes 'Is this for the benefit of cricket?' as distinct from 'Is this for the benefit of me?'

The code of conduct derives from an implied notion of

service to intrinsic satisfactions of the game, which is a voluntary contest of skills within agreed rules. Opponents are equally entitled to satisfactions if they can earn them, therefore breaking the rules and advantage gained by cheating come under disapproval. Breach of rule incurs a stipulated penalty; cheating incurs opprobrium. The morality of cricket has said that protection of the wicket with the pads is, in certain circumstances, illegal and subject to a punishment of law. The batsman is out, l.b.w. These were terms on which batsman and bowler undertook the contest. The morality of cricket has also said that to derive advantage by misrepresentation of the law is cheating. Punishment for claiming catches the claimant knows to have been picked up on the half-volley is a reputation for poor sportsmanship. The terms of participation assume equal opportunity to both sides, or contestants, for achieving the game's satisfactions.

In summary, everybody is expected to 'play fair', to the benefit of the game and all its players. Human nature being what it is everybody did not play fair all the time, but lapses were forgiven rather than defended.

Principles can change with purposes. Ploughshares can be turned into swords. Once the function of sport as an end in itself comes to be questioned the values and acceptable conduct of sport tend to be reassessed. The 'done thing' may cease to be done; sportsmanship may need a revised definition.

Advance the argument that sport at first-class level is more than sport; is a commercial venture; is a political concern; is a personal promotion and you instigate different concepts of the permissible. Art, you could proclaim, is properly a handmaiden to advertisement; success is the heart-beat of survival; the rewards of talent are measured by the bank account.

From this viewpoint sport is not its own justification. It acquires ulterior motives. First-class cricket and League football are business propositions. The Olympic Games are exploitation of national assets. Players are essentially making a living for themselves. Sport is a means to ends beyond itself.

Given such premise, to prevent an Association goal by a Rugby tackle is not cheating; it is a business necessity. Drug-taking to run faster or jump higher than anyone else becomes dutiful in a country's cause. Controversial behaviour induces profitable notoriety.

Sooner or later irreconcilable philosophies must part company and isolate themselves in separate territories. In some games the division has apparently taken place. Principles and practices recognized at first-class level are not principles and practices applicable to lower levels; the superior few have moved into a rarefied atmosphere. The first-class players, managements, exploiters do not live in the general world any longer; they could, no doubt, step down occasionally to join us but we cannot visit them.

Cricket, I feel, has still to experience the vital severance. A hazy borderland remains. The higher reaches are clearly moving towards a commercial and political environment, with county cricket shaped as an advertising package and international cricket commanded by a government department. Individuals, guided by professional agents, are leaning towards an attitude that asserts the game should be devised and directed primarily to meet their requirements. To this end there is a players' organization and there are demands for the widest freedom of action in contracts that are unenforceable by one party. On the one hand is the security expressed in a long engagement; on the other is the impracticality of an unwilling player.

It is easy enough to envisage first-class cricket of the future being entirely commercial, presented and paid for as an advertising medium. In that event, publicity-value would be the criterion of success. The cause to be served would not be the cause of cricket as a game but the cause of promotion, just as the cause of televised cricket is, basically, not cricket but a television show.

For cricket the game and cricket the commercial concern different sets of values are raised. In one context an explosion of temper on the field is bad for cricket and therefore to be deprecated, but in another context it may be good publicity and therefore accepted. A match won by blatant sharp practice would be of little satisfaction by some canons of cricket but could, through the result, be of deep commercial significance.

In simple illustration, deliberate time-wasting in a friendly game of club cricket would please no one and would be frowned on because the purpose of play is lost to players and spectators alike. The same tactics employed to win a championship or a Test rubber could be defended as justifiable means to a profitable end.

This is not academic theory. It has happened and it is happening. It has been seen in Test and county cricket. It is seen week by week in Association football of first-class standard. It is seen in tournament golf when a slow competitor takes five or six hours to complete a round, to the frustration of the playing partner and the fury of those waiting behind.

Where the commercial becomes completely separated from the recreational differences in approach and conduct are created. The unacceptable in one can become tolerable, even approved, in the other. Difficulties arise in the period of separation, when the differing moralities are not crystallized and impinge on both areas. The recreational golfer, taking a lead from the tournament golfer, assumes slow play to be meritorious and exasperates a whole membership. Committees have to issue a directive and those reproved are probably both indignant and puzzled. First-class cricketers find themselves confusingly applauded for victory in matches that also provoke reprimand for misconduct. The schoolboy footballer notes foul play by his hero acknowledged as virtuous and, naturally, reproduces it without shame in his own context.

The individual player finds himself struggling with divided

loyalties. His heart may tell him to 'play the game', scorning any unfair advantage, but his head reminds him that not only his own immediate welfare but also that of a team may be best served by the end-product of, say, winning or protesting or even declining to play.

Similar reaction is transferable to spectators and followers. Satisfactions derive less from the play than from the ultimate success of a player or a team supported. Distraction and disruption directed against the opposition or the controlling authority comes to be regarded as both customary and laudable.

Cricket, I think and hope, is not yet irrevocably committed to the final division between recreational sport and commercial entertainment. The trend is obvious enough because the first-class level has grown increasingly dependent on commercial sponsorship and government subsidy and the presentation of play has been adjusted to meet requirements. Leading players have indicated changing views on self-exploitation; crowd response and behaviour have been re-channelled.

There are, however, signs of recognition that the ultimate separation would be self-destructive. Cricket as commercial entertainment is a selling proposition to sponsors, to television and to the public only when it displays first-class cricketers. It is their skills and their reputations that form the attraction and it is becoming realized that unless the skills and reputations can be acquired the supply of goods for sale will be reduced.

The chain of development linking all cricket is logical. Club cricket can produce only club cricketers; the best of them want the something more that is first-class cricket; the best of first-class cricketers become the Test players, renowned and respected as ideals for all cricketers. If ever the attraction of the stage beyond club cricket should lose its appeal to all cricketers the binding chain would break.

I believe the chain would break if cricket at various levels became imbued with different aims and purposes and codes of conduct. The separate sections might exist and flourish each in its own environment, but the commercial entertainment section would be highly vulnerable to fashions in finance, political influence and the aspect of public fancy that favours material success above all else.

My hope for the future of cricket lies in those cricketers who will always seek widening satisfactions from the game itself. They will ensure the common purpose at all levels of play; they will seek dissemination of common principles from inspiration and example at the top; they will insist on cricket independence.

13. Leaders in Opposition

Cricket is a team game of individual encounter. It is a team game in aspects of fieldsmen helping bowlers and partners helping batsmen and, of course, in attitudes of play that demand self-subjugation and sometimes self-sacrifice; but the bowler in delivery, the batsman taking strike, must rely entirely on themselves. No colleague can direct a batsman's stroke, no allied force can strengthen a bowler's arm.

Cricket needs teams for realization of its widest potential, but the essence of the game can be distilled by two players, one bowling and one batting. In that context, presumably cricket was born and the early 'champions' were those successful in the direct contest of single-wicket matches.

Through all its development to sophistication cricket has retained the element of personal encounter. The great players meeting hand-to-hand are the heart-beat of attraction. Seen, they are summits of delight; imagined, they are the material for epics. If only Barnes could have bowled to Grace, Spofforth to Hobbs, Alfred Shaw to Bradman; what cricket then would have been created, what marvels from the matching of the matchless.

In the narrower bounds of actuality there has been abundant glory of individual encounter. By the chance of time and place and circumstance great personal antagonisms have arisen to blaze across the pages of history. I mean antagonism in the technical medium, for, as far as I know, the great cricketing rivalries have been confined to playing hours and have increased rather than diminished mutual respect and regard. I have every reason to suppose that Sir Leonard Hutton and R.R.Lindwall would happily share the same dining-table, though theirs was an outstanding conflict in cricket.

They knew of each other before they met. But for war Hutton would have been in Australia before 1946, carrying the grace and burden of his innings of 364. Delay increased Australian desire to see and measure his batting and Australian resolve to balance the books. When cricket came back Hutton was an inevitable Australian target for concentrated attack.

Lindwall came into first-class cricket, for New South Wales, in 1945 and murmurs of his quality penetrated England. During preparations for the M.C.C. tour I remember Hutton observing: 'They say there's a chap called Lindwall who is good and pretty quick.' No doubt there was also a thought in Lindwall's mind of a chap called Hutton being good and pretty persistent.

I confess that I missed the significance of Lindwall on my first sight of him, but I console myself with a reflection that the introduction was scarcely a sight at all. It was in a match ruined by rain and poor light; Lindwall bowled little and without showing his best pace and I remarked an unclassically low arm rather than a classically smooth run-up.

Second impressions were much more powerful; I came to relish Lindwall as one of the greatest of fast bowlers and to appreciate his personal duels with Hutton as cricket in its finest hours. The two scarcely came to grips in the Brisbane Test where Hutton was bowled by Miller for seven in the first innings and Lindwall retired with chicken-pox before the end of the match; but through the series the gage of challenge was clearly thrown down.

Figures misrepresent the outcome. Hutton scored 417 in Tests and was dismissed by Lindwall, who took eighteen wickets, only once; but Hutton knew and Lindwall knew and everyone watching knew of battle joined by protagonists of exceptional significance.

An ultimate authority was never established. At no time could, or did, Lindwall regard Hutton as an anonymous batsman, to be challenged with a routine attack in the circumstances of the occasion; at no time could Hutton contemplate Lindwall as 'just another bowler'. In their individual confrontations there was always a tension that elevated the standards of contest. It was typified in the grim silence of understanding that followed 'Hutton b. Lindwall 0' in a first over at Headingley in 1953. It was typified in the long hauls to 145 at Lord's when Lindwall was taking five other wickets and to 156 not out at Adelaide after Lindwall had broken into an innings that totalled no more than 272.

Perhaps the balance was illustrated to perfection at the Oval in 1948 when Lindwall swept away the England batting for a total of fifty-two. Hutton made thirty by beautiful and flawless batting and was last man out—to Lindwall—caught from a legitimate leg-glance by a diving wicketkeeper.

Hutton and Lindwall were fascinating in direct opposition because they drew the best from each other in a wide range of technique. Lindwall never allowed Hutton to 'bat in his sleep'; Hutton never permitted Lindwall the relaxation of mechanical 'bread and butter' bowling. Hutton knew that he must always expect any variation from the swinging yorker to the swift bumper. Lindwall knew that drive, cut and glance were awaiting every opportunity for display. Unceasing thoughtfulness was always evident in both batsman and bowler.

Respect was deep but it was not measured in any terms of merciful dispensation. If Lindwall thought Hutton could be disturbed by a barrage of bumpers then bumpers would fly. If Hutton thought Lindwall could be reduced to hands-and-knees weariness no consolatory concession would be offered. Each counted subjection of the other the highest personal satisfaction to be derived from a team responsibility. They presented a purely cricketing antagonism that raised excitement and admiration in all of us.

Over a shorter period and in rather less exacting circumstances, but equally as thrilling in prospect and experience, were the contests between Woolley and E.A.McDonald. Both were supreme artists in their particular medium, each could be touched to magnificence by the challenge of the other.

Their most memorable hours of opposition were not in Test matches because in McDonald's brief Test career Australia held an overwhelming supremacy. Less was demanded in expectation of McDonald than of Lindwall, of Woolley than of Hutton. Woolley did play some splendid innings when McDonald was bowling for Australia, but none of them was decisive in a match. In eight Tests McDonald took Woolley's wicket only twice, each time to raise Australian relief more than jubilation.

Representing Kent and Lancashire Woolley and McDonald became much more dominating figures in opposition. They were clearly the champions in their sphere. By overcoming McDonald Woolley could open doors to a Kent victory; dismissing Woolley McDonald could tumble Kent to defeat.

These enthralling possibilities became actuality. McDonald and Woolley opposed their splendours and decided issues. Outstanding encounters were seen by Cardus and described by him in the glow of witness. The facts and figures are in *Wisden*. No more can be done to arrange the bones and clothe with living flesh and anyone who ever saw McDonald bowl and Woolley bat must know that cricket could offer no finer sight than the one against the other, with all to play for.

McDonald the bowler was menacing in appearance, sardonic in manner and inclined to be fatalistic in temperament. Of all fast bowlers his was surely the most beautiful action. His run-up was long but not excessive and it was a glide not a pounding charge. On dry turf he could bowl twenty overs without leaving a footprint and the whole approach, delivery and follow-through was so smooth that it seemed to have no beginning and no end.

Analysed, his bowling was full of technical expertise, with the necessary variations for outswing, inswing and subtle change of pace, but to general observation his artistry concealed art. When the pitch was soft or the fires of fast bowling burned low in his mood he would bowl off-breaks at medium pace, competently accumulating a store of success that amounted to 720 wickets in four successive Lancashire seasons.

In his fast bowling he scattered inadequate opposition with imperious contempt. 'This unequal contest,' said his swift yorker or break-back, 'should not be prolonged.' There are three hat-tricks to his name and three times he took three wickets in four balls. The greater batsmen, particularly in conditions favourable to batting, or the critical hour invoked his inspiration or roused his bowling wrath. He could threaten heads or rap fingers on the most placid pitch.

Pit him, therefore, against Woolley, by whom speed was measured as the ball left the bat not as it left the bowler, and cricketing magnificence was assured; elegance matching elegance, power meeting power, protagonist acknowledging protagonist. There was no holding back by either party, no quest for discreet maiden by the bowler, no tactical restraint or retreat by the batsman. McDonald bowled to dismiss Woolley instantly; Woolley batted to dispatch McDonald forthwith. Each had his way at one time or another and cricket found a greater glory for their having had a chance to meet.

A later generation experienced comparable delight when Trueman was in the lists with Peter May. Here again was fast bowling and batting of the highest class, here again the individual challenge recognized by both batsman and bowler. May and Trueman were colleagues as often as they were opponents, each rejoiced in the success of the other against a common enemy, regard was mutual and sincere. The respect they exchanged was a spur to endeavour when they were thrown into single combat.

They faced each other as champions. May was more than a representative of Surrey's batting; through the long championship reign he was the bulk of it, prop and stay as well as decoration. May carried both the banner and the rations for

Surrey and without his runs Laker, Lock and Bedser would have been deprived of half their bowling scope.

Trueman's responsibility was precisely parallel. For season after season he was Yorkshire's only match-winning bowler. When he was resting Yorkshire in the field looked a workaday side, waiting for a turn of fortune. When he was in activity expectations invariably ran high.

May and Trueman understood their relative significance well enough. If Trueman dismissed May his whole attitude, and probably his voice, said 'Done thi' in tones of infinite satisfaction. If May drove a beautiful boundary, or stopped a yorker or evaded a bumper his shy half-smile indicated 'One to me, Fred.' They relished the battle even more deeply than it was relished by spectators, for in committed crowds there is a blood-lust that sometimes obscures the splendour of battle itself. Trueman appreciated the great batsmanship in May and concentrated all his effort and skill to overcome it. May saw and sensed the Trueman endeavour and artistry and responded with inspiration that illuminated his own ability.

No doubt statisticians could strike a balance of relative achievement, could evaluate performances of runs scored and the wicket taken to balls bowled, rate early dismissals and centuries completed. Whatever the figures indicate I am prepared to set them aside in happy recollection of great bowling and great batting fascinatingly matched without need for determination of superiority. The highest compliment I can offer to both is my conviction that each was worthy challenger for the other.

Great fast bowling opposed to great batting must represent the most thrilling of personal encounters because of the manifest physical element, but the student observer can derive long-lasting satisfaction from skilled batting meeting the subtleties of slow bowling. Victor Trumper and Wilfred Rhodes created a day of classic contest at Sydney and above all his other experiences in cricket Hedley Verity placed bowling to Bradman.

Bradman's batting achievements and reputation were so enormous that every bowler counted him a special enemy, though few ever thought of him as an adversary on equal terms. Everyone hoped to defeat him; only the supremely self-confident expected to do so.

Verity was among the self-confident. Without arrogance, without vanity he made no secret of his desire to bowl against Bradman at any time in any conditions. This to him was the summit of bowling challenge and he wished to express himself on the heights of his art.

He did not crave the favour of the pitch every time. He was glad of it in the Lord's Test of 1934 when he took fourteen wickets, harassing Bradman to swift suicide, but he recognized imbalance of opportunity and in his heart of bowling hearts he preferred the contest wherein a conquest had to be planned and devised with patient unfolding of skills. He wanted to beat Bradman in circumstances where Bradman had a fair chance to belabour him.

The circumstances were provided. The Test matches of the 1930s were played more often on good pitches than on bad and Verity expected to have to bowl thirty overs in most Australian innings. They were invariably overs of thoughtful relation one to another, overs of accumulating pressure and significance. Verity bowled in the unshakable belief that, sooner or later, he would dismiss Bradman in the way he intended to dismiss him. He had his disappointments in such Bradman scores as 304 at Headingley, 244 at the Oval, 270 at Melbourne, 212 at Adelaide and 144 not out at Trent Bridge, but belief never wavered. Verity was genuinely sorry when Bradman had to miss a Test match.

Once, at Melbourne in 1937, Verity came on to take Bradman's wicket with the first ball he sent down. The bowler was almost disappointed. The catch at short leg was too much in the nature of a batting accident for Verity to savour full satisfaction. His were pleasures in the longer term, pleasures of the great opponent harassed to a final mishit or lulled to an error of momentary over-assurance. Verity wanted to work for Bradman's wicket, to develop a plan, to watch the closing of a trap. At Sydney he opened a gateway to ready scoring in the belief that one small footmark near the line of the leg stump would enable him to turn the ball past an eager bat. At Lord's he cleared a pathway to the third-man boundary and persuaded an inside-edge on to the stumps.

Whether or not Bradman ever devoted such concentration on Verity's bowling as Verity on Bradman's batting only the players involved could know, but the appreciation of each for the other was as plain as the resolution to challenge was splendid and fascinating. Figures show only what the interpreter cares to make of them. In sixteen Test-match meetings Verity took Bradman's wicket eight times and Bradman made eight centuries. Honours were not so much divided as added together, bowling enhanced by the power in the batting and batting elevated by the skill and persistence in the bowling.

Verity and Bradman made opposition in the epic mould, the gods in contention. Yorkshire's Maurice Leyland and J.W.A.Stephenson of Essex matched themselves in merriment. Theirs was a contest of serious skills cloaked in cap and bells. They were designed by nature to be friendly enemies, the phlegmatic professional with an amateur sense of fun and the volatile amateur with a professional dedication and appreciation.

Leyland was a highly accomplished batsman, tempered in Test-match fires, and an occasional bowler of imagination and unorthodox spin. Stephenson was a fast-medium bowler, menacing with the new ball, indefatigable with the old, and a lower-order batsman always eager for an innings. The talents were ideally opposed. Leyland had the batting ability and reputation to make a Stephenson bowling conquest a matter for uninhibited Stephenson joy. Leyland's wicket was no commonplace capture and as Leyland readily acknowledged the citadel had not been lightly conceded. Stephenson was pleased and he had to say so. After an exultant leap he entered into mutual congratulation with the wicketkeeper and the slips and sometimes with deep square leg. After all it was not every day that Stephenson—or anybody else—defeated a Leyland.

There were, of course, days on which Stephenson did not defeat Leyland, but the attempt itself made a day's joy. Stephenson relished the battle and so did Leyland, and honest respect underlay the inter-overs exchange of banter. When Stephenson came in to bat Leyland invariably asked to be allowed to bowl. His 'chinamen' sometimes deceived reputable batsmen; they never failed to bewilder Stephenson.

The harassed batsman would plunge forward to the peril of his trousers seams; he would scramble back in a tangle of boots and bat; as often as not he would depart with all the disbelief of a victim of the three-card trick and Leyland would turn to the umpire for his sweater, business concluded.

Fellow-players, spectators on the boundary and participants all enjoyed the comedy. The high endeavour and the obvious good nature in the contest communicated themselves to command rapt attention. Leyland and Stephenson were clearly striving to the utmost of their ability and the outcome of their challenge was the most important thing in the world—until it had been decided. Then it became no more than a happy memory for both of the contestants and all observers; who bowled out whom was of no further significance, but the contending remained a treasure of sport beyond the corruption of moth or the intrusion of thieves.

14. Footsteps

The Page is not the heroic figure in the story of Good King Wenceslas but presumably, in his later consideration of the Stephen's Day adventure, he preened himself a little in terms of association. In his master's steps he trod. I can appreciate his feelings because I can reproduce them, faintly, in a claim to have shared a cricketing experience with Alfred Mynn.

Justification for the vanity demands a flight of fancy and must acknowledge that others may share, but there cannot be many of us left.

Alfred Mynn died in 1861. He played his cricket in the Middle Ages of the game's history, before development of the county framework and before the transformation wrought by W.G.Grace. Mynn was the 'champion' of his time, less widely renowned than the champion of all times, but titled by his specific achievement in winning six open challenge matches on single-wicket terms. In contemporary cricket status, as in physical stature, Mynn and Grace were comparable giants.

Alfred Mynn was born and bred in rural Kent and came to cricket in the natural course of sporting activities. Physique and temperament offered him primary advantages. His height in manhood was well above six feet, his weight without superfluity of flesh was eighteen stones and he had exceptional strength of arm and shoulder. His temper was smooth and he was of the friendliest disposition, with a trusting simplicity that made him both a ready pupil and a vulnerable subject for exploitation.

Without tuition the young giant might have remained a tearaway cricketer of no more than local significance, but a patron who was also an experienced player appreciated possibilities and became instructor. He was the John Willes who had been directly involved in controversy created by the introduction of round-arm bowling as successor to the underarm delivery of early custom. Willes, a man of means and spirit, was a first-rank player who cast himself out of metropolitan cricket after being no-balled for the new 'throwing' at Lord's. From self-imposed exile to his Kent village Willes noted inviting material for a coach in the fearsome bowling of Alfred Mynn.

The untutored Mynn hurled the ball at great pace from a long run-up but he gave away more runs in wides than were justified by wickets taken. Under guidance and through sustained practice the pace was preserved and accuracy acquired from a stately approach of six paces that became an identification, like the walking stride of Wilfred Rhodes or the leap of J.M.Gregory.

Mynn's repute widened from the villages of Kent to the full range of cricket in England. He played for the Gentlemen against the Players at Lord's; he represented Kent and the South against the North; and in his later career he became a leading figure in the peripatetic All-England Eleven devised by William Clarke.

Mynn was more than a testing fast bowler. He was an accomplished batsman, powerful as would be expected in straight driving and hitting to leg. In a period when the individual century was a rarity he scored 125 not out for the South against the North and in innumerable smaller innings he set the course of a match or turned it. He fulfilled the qualification a true all-rounder in justifying selection as a bowler without batting or as a batsman without bowling.

With such capacity Mynn's success in single-wicket challenge is not surprising. Fast bowling and straight driving suited the terms of man-to-man contest. By the rules of the time the bowler had the assistance of only two fieldsmen, but the batsman was severely restricted in scoring range because he could not leave his crease to play a stroke and he could score only from hits in front of the wicket. The late cut, the leg-glance, the hook behind square were all wasted effort. A single run was the equivalent of two in double-wicket terms because the batsman had to run to the bowling wicket and back to his own crease to count one. No-balls and wides, each counting only one, were added to his total.

Scoring was usually low and slow. Alfred Mynn won an innings victory in one challenge match with a score of five, yet the game involved almost a whole day's play. In the six matches that gave him his title of 'Champion of England' only once did Mynn the bowler concede more than nine runs in an innings. Mynn the hard-driving batsman had scores of 88, 46, 33 and 32 to emphasize his all-round superiority.

A player may receive appreciation for outstanding performance without winning general public esteem. Alfred Mynn captured hearts as well as heads. The very sight of his handsome face and magnificent figure was an attraction and his companionable manner gave him wide popularity among both players and patrons. He himself was a patron of beef and beer and he consumed cheerfully and prodigiously at any table. In his personal finances he was careless to a point of irresponsibility and he missed some cricketing engagements because of imprisonment for debt, but there is no suggestion that he ever succumbed to the bribery that was commonplace in the cricket of his time.

Alfred Mynn was always nominally an amateur player, but he followed no other profession with sufficient persistence to ensure a livelihood and presumably he drew an indecisive line between match-expenses and fees. Much of his cricket was under the open patronage of admirers and when he joined the All-England tours he received payment, if not for playing then for rather vague administrative responsibilities.

In Clarke's team Mynn was unquestionably both a playing and a social asset. The All-England side originated in 1846 when Mynn was thirty-nine years old and past his best on the field, the mighty muscles weakening and mobility decreasing, but his was the appearance most frequently requested when fixtures were being planned, his the company most eagerly sought when players and supporters mingled.

The All-England organization was a commercial venture. Most of the matches were absurdly unbalanced as contests in cricket and Mynn was not often required to stretch his talents on the field, but All-England visits made feast-days for local cricket and in the social undertakings he was in every sense an outstanding figure.

In 1847 the team played in Sheffield and were due at Newcastle-upon-Tyne a few days later. To occupy the intervening time they were invited to stay and play at Wentworth Woodhouse, the South Yorkshire home of the Earls Fitzwilliam. The specific host was the eldest son of the family, Lord Milton, who had played against the All-England Eleven in the Sheffield match.

From contemporary accounts the house-party seems to have been conspicuously successful.

> The hospitable board of the noble earl [says the magazine *Bell's Life*] groaned beneath every substantial delicacy of the season. . . . Throughout each day Earl Fitzwilliam, the Honourable Ladies and a string of company occupied chairs upon the lawn and there was a considerable number of visitors who ranged themselves around the scene of action. The lawn is in front of the house and comprises between fourteen and fifteen acres of beautiful turf. This spot has been devoted by the noble earl to the purposes of cricket.

Nearly eighty years later a schoolboy of no renown at all followed Alfred Mynn on to the same wide lawn for purposes of cricket. I, too, was welcomed into Wentworth Woodhouse for changing-room accommodation and refreshment. Perhaps I prepared for cricket where Alfred Mynn had once prepared, sat at the same long table—though I fancy our beverages were different. No snow lay dinted but I must certainly have trodden near Mynn's footsteps along the paths and down the wide steps to the lawn that was still kept for purposes of cricket. Another Lord Milton was playing for Wentworth Woodhouse.

This one, if memory serves, was an Eton schoolboy at the time. I have no remaining impression of his cricketing consequence, nor of the general course of the match, but I do remember a moment of personal bewilderment. I was bowling when a bearded batsman of senior status came to the wicket. He took guard and surveyed the field in customary manner before assuming a conventional stance, but as I began my run-up he stood upright, lifting his bat shoulder-high and throwing back his head as though to look far behind me.

I stopped, presuming he was not ready, and returned to my mark. Seeing him in a normal stance I began my run-up again, but again he stood up, head lifted so that his brown beard pointed towards me, his eyes apparently searching the outfield. I thought there must be some distraction behind me, but, turning, I could find no wandering fieldsman or spectator in the line of vision. We started again.

After a third abortive attempt to proceed with play the batsman spoke. 'Come on,' he said. 'It's all right; I'm ready.'

In later disclosure I learned that I had bowled to the Fitzwilliam estate agent, whose cricket enthusiasm was not too daunted by a handicap in eyesight. How comfortably he dealt with my schoolboy bowling on the Wentworth Woodhouse lawn I cannot remember, but I imagine he would have found more difficulty in the 'fast, ripping' square-arm challenge of Alfred Mynn in the same impressive setting.

15. In the 1950s

The division of cricket between the wars and cricket in its present guise is to be found in the 1950s rather than in the war years themselves. The resumed cricket of 1946 was cricket of 1939 in conception, eagerly and happily taken up again with an awareness of shortcomings expected to be temporary, but with no anticipation of fundamental change. For a few years the game blossomed in nostalgia.

Crowds were never bigger, public interest was never higher. Touring teams took home unparalleled profits and Old Trafford had to close gates when Yorkshire were the visiting team. Bradman became Sir Donald and international development spread with no more disturbance than occasional pin-pricks on surface harmony. Cricket was seen in the light of its 1939 character; a game presented as a public entertainment.

In the first seasons of resumption satisfactions of relief glossed over inescapable inconveniences and improvisations. England was still on utility standards. Food was rationed; petrol was rationed; materials were in short supply. Most of the country, certainly its cricket grounds, looked shabby and most of the people, including newcomers to county cricket, had of necessity to look makeshift in attire.

Travel between engagements was slow and uncomfortable because train services were inadequate and the use of private cars was restricted. Coach journeys frequently extended far into the night, elongated by diversion to widely scattered homes within a county. Sleeping and eating raised problems, with hotels crowded to compel room-sharing and dinner tables were rarely able to offer more than a statutory five-shilling meal.

Spectatorial amenities had deteriorated under war-time neglect and damage and though county authorities were willing to spend they found frustration in building regulations and priorities. Houses were needed before dressing-rooms, schools and hospitals required the timber and steel and paint that cricket clubs sought for pavilions, enclosures and seating—to say nothing of refreshment rooms and toilets.

Yet cricket flourished. It was relished thankfully by those who had known it before the Interruption, approached eagerly by a new generation of the ambitious and accepted as a social adornment through the exceptionally warm and sunny summers of 1947 and 1949 and the exciting season of 1948 that brought Bradman on his farewell tour.

The time stays typified for me in recollection of an August afternoon in 1947 at the Dean Park ground in Bournemouth. The match was of little significance in the championship, for neither Hampshire nor Yorkshire could reach the head of the table, but the golden weather, the holiday period and the presence of great players had drawn a crowd too big for the seating capacity but uncomplainingly spread across the grass, among the marquees and in the shade of trees and high boundary hedges.

There was a little folding of the hands among the senior spectators, occasional restlessness among the sun-bronzed juveniles who had long since disposed of sustenance brought for lunch and tea, but a general air of attentiveness and appreciation for the polished performances on show. The cricket and the occasion were being enjoyed.

In my peregrinations I had come across an Australian journalist, Tom Goodman, who was making his first visit to England on a year's commission to cover Australian interests in Rugby League football and cricket tours. At Bournemouth he was an uncommitted spectator, observing and absorbing the practices and atmosphere of county cricket. We stood in the crowd, considering the general scene rather than details of play; our panoramic view ranged from the little pavilion on our left to tented enclosures on the far side of the ground. The weather was warm enough to meet Australian requirements, but the essence of the occasion was wholly English. The huge arenas of Sydney and Melbourne, with their towering stands and railed-off, regimented sections of spectators, were literally more than half the world away. The cricket, for all the schoolboy cries, the ripples of applause, the ceaseless murmur of comment, had a restfulness of routine understood and appreciated. In one hour of one afternoon Tom Goodman enjoyed an experience that all the scorecards and the record-books could not have given.

This enjoyment was not lessened for me by familiarity. In a long association with county cricket I have been granted innumerable days of quiet satisfaction in the routine of the game, days without dramatic incident, days on which the quality of play and the patina of place created a pleasurable background to events without any historic significance. Such days I counted the essence of first-class cricket, a conglomerate impression to be treasured in memory and desired in anticipation. Happily for me, in my particular professional assignments, I could indulge romantic reverie as readily at Bradford as at Brighton, at Middlesbrough and at Maidstone.

I certainly passed happily and hopefully into the cricket of the 1950s. As far as I knew at the time the cricket I cared for was re-creating itself in an accepted pattern. Observation could not avoid a deterioration in standards of technical expertise and professional responsibility among recruits, but there was sympathetic regard for players who had been deprived of basic cricket education at school and club level and allowance had to be made for time lost to compulsory military service.

The critical misgivings of the 1950s were not directed towards standards shown by the leading players, but towards a widening gap between the few and the many and the apparent complacency of the many in their lower estate. Among the few there was evidence of exceptional talent and its development was exciting. Sometimes it was over-exciting and the history of the period is littered with geese briefly mistaken for swans, but a decade that brought to the mature splendours of Hutton and Compton and Washbrook an infusion of Bedser, Evans, May, Cowdrey, Trueman and the meteoric Tyson could not have been a degradation in cricket.

The 1950s gave me enthralling experiences. They were the years of Bedser's magnificence in bowling and I, brought up on Barnes and Tate, had standards for the recognition of greatness and for rejoicing in it. I have never been more absorbed in an art, more enchained in the atmosphere of an occasion, than at Trent Bridge in 1953 when Bedser took seven wickets in each Australian innings.

Each time the need was pressing and the achievement was dramatic. In the first innings the Australians fell from 237 for four to 249 all out under the second new ball. In the second Australian innings Bedser was bowling to an England overdraft of 105 runs. In his first effort Bedser kept England in the match; by his second effort he gave his side a chance of victory.

On the two afternoons of his tremendous attack the setting might have been designed for Wagnerian opera. The sky was overcast, the air was heavy with moisture and the bowling successes raised a tremble of wonder and anticipation in the crowd. The most casual and unsophisticated of spectators could not have avoided involvement. The cricket was to be felt as well as seen. When intervals came the relief from tension was needed by watchers as well as by players.

The silence of absorbed attention carried Bedser through his run-up of balanced stride and rocking shoulders. Sigh or sharp cry of acclamation pursued the consequence of almost every stroke. Over by over swelled recognition of the impossible being realized. Fielding was inspired to hold swirling catches even when they had been misjudged. Bedser was captain of his soul, master of his fate and, apparently, director of the cricketing fates themselves.

All through his career, in days of triumph or frustration, Bedser was manifestly a bowler of quality. He never neglected the basics which proclaim that a straight, good-length bowler is a good bowler. Bedser invariably maintained length and direction. To make himself outstanding he mastered swing and 'cut', presented, or inflicted, at lively medium pace. His leg-cutter which reversed the inswinging line of flight was virtually beyond counter by orthodox practices of batsmanship. It was delivered to perfection in the Trent Bridge Test of 1953 and Hassett, bowled when his score was 115, claimed high skill in 'getting a touch' before his off stump was uprooted. Bradman, clean bowled for nought at Adelaide, acknowledged that he had never been more comprehensively defeated in his batting experience.

Bedser made three tours of Australia as a player and in the second one he took thirty-nine wickets in the five Tests. In the home series of 1953 he took the same number and, even against the challenge of Lindwall, he could fairly be rated first among the great bowlers of his time.

Dethronement, in Test-match terms, came during the third tour. Few bowlers have been able to sustain success over a third tour, but on the outward voyage of 1954 there was general anticipation that Bedser would be the mainstay of England's bowling, as he had been for almost a decade. Suffering from shingles he missed the early matches and when he played, perhaps not fully fit, in the first Test at Brisbane he shared the bowling discomfiture reflected in an Australian total of 601.

He was dropped for the second Test—logically enough by current form and performances, but controversially in the particular circumstances and manner of omission. The first morning of the Sydney Test provided an atmosphere of high humidity and a pitch with dampness in it, the precise conditions to suit Bedser's type of bowling, though in fact he would have been denied opportunity because Australia won the toss and made England bat. Hutton and the selectors had already decided on a policy-revision in which there was no scope for Bedser, as there had been none for Tate in Jardine's design of 1932–3. The conditions of the Sydney morning raised a complication that left Hutton open to criticism, but he was giving precedence to a policy over an improvisation and events justified his judgement.

In the details of his omission Bedser may have been rather tactlessly treated. A story circulated that only publication of the team-sheet told him he would not be playing and if this be so I think Bedser deserved kindlier treatment. His service was too long and honourable for its end to be indicated without consolatory explanation. All cricketers are overtaken when their stride begins to flag in the march of time, but the fall-out of the great ones should surely be eased whenever possible.

The 1950s gave more than a model of fast-medium bowling in Bedser. They gave splendid illustration of almost every type of style of bowling and batting. In English cricket no left-handed batsman of the highest rank emerged—though one ought to have done under the name of Brian Close—and there was little leg-break bowling of quality, but all the other arts of cricket were on show.

Principles of classical batsmanship were handed on from Hutton and Compton to May and Cowdrey. Comparisons of merit would be fruitless and irrelevant, but few observers of the period would deny a blood brotherhood of the four in batting quality. They all wore the purple and would have done in any age of cricket. Cowdrey in self-confidence evoked pictures of Hammond, with majesty on the off-side and time in hand when the ball was turning. At his best he was the most easeful batsman of his time and even in his introspective innings he never looked less than an England player.

May, I shall always believe, came close to being a director of cricket, as Grace and Hobbs were directors. Grace put fast bowling in its place. He broke its threatened dominance, left it an essential part of the game but not the controlling influence. Grace's batting widened the scope of batsmanship and consequently of cricket.

Hobbs also took batting a step further than he found it. But for his swift and masterful reponse googly bowling might have spread an overwhelming infection. There was fast bowling after Grace, there was googly bowling after Hobbs, but they were aspects of bowling, not the whole of it, because Grace and Hobbs demonstrated the batting counter and those who noted were able to follow.

Had May stayed a little longer on the fields I think his example could have established a school of batting attitude to turn the tide of inslant bowling that flooded first-class cricket and left it a more restricted game and a less attractive public entertainment. May was a batsman of wide range, but more than anyone of his period he ventured into the on-drive against inswing or off-break bowling. Accurate footwork and confident approach enabled him to force the ball between mid-on and mid-wicket where so many of his contemporaries were reduced to a cramped defensive stroke or a tentative leg-glance. May hit the leg-side half-volleys from an upright stance and with a full swing of the bat that gave both power and beauty.

I hoped he would be followed by eager young batsmen inspired by his method and achievement, with the ultimate result of bowling patterns changing simply on grounds of unprofitability. I think he might have been, but for the sad shortening of his own career and but for the spread of one-day cricket that has stultified first-class thinking and development.

Whatever my fancy and reasoning, Peter May would certainly not have considered his own batting as evangelistic. His talent and his career thrust greatness upon him but he accepted it more from a sense of responsibility than a desire to command and rebuild his cricketing world. His most magnificent shots were followed by a downward gaze, as of embarrassment; when he had been beaten or forced into hasty defence he made acknowledgement with a shy smile for the bowler.

He crowded enormous effort into a short first-class career, carrying the burden of England captaincy, at home and abroad, through forty-one Tests in six years. He was the foundation and much of the superstructure in Surrey's batting during an unparalleled run of championship success. He was under pressing demand for festival and benefit matches. His failures made headlines and his successes invaded the personal privacy he desired so earnestly.

Exhausted, he left cricket too soon for cricket's good, but he could not be accused of desertion. He had given of himself without stint and left an unfading glory. Nobody playing or watching in the period of Peter May could complain that the time was without greatness.

May himself would no doubt agree, but he would point the finger elsewhere, insisting that the 1950s were primarily bowling and fielding years. The records of his country and county support the thesis. In England selection committee meetings the hours were spent in finding batsmen but choosing between bowlers. Statham, Trueman and Tyson were contemporaries and Loader went twice to Australia. Lock and Wardle were alternatives in left-arm spin and Laker was not the only off-spinner to be considered—though on technical merit his claims were surely indisputable. Appleyard had attributes of greatness, but was granted too little time to exploit them.

Bob Appleyard's potential was no sooner seen than it was confirmed. In his first full season for Yorkshire he took 200 wickets. In the next summer, 1952, he fell ill and was compelled to undergo extensive sanatorium treatment before returning to cricket to take 141 wickets for Yorkshire in 1954 and earn himself a place in Hutton's team touring Australia. With limited opportunity he took eleven Test wickets on the tour, but ill-health and injuries forced him out of cricket all too soon.

Appleyard's bowling was basically off-spin at medium pace, but he cultivated pace variations that made him uncommonly difficult to play, or to define. Time and again batsmen in forward defence found themselves bowled with the stroke half-completed. Appleyard was tall and bowled with a high arm and because of the 'bounce' he obtained he made forcing shots speculative.

In manner of bowling he was patently antagonistic and he was never satisfied with himself. After he had reached Test status I chanced upon him at Headingley one April afternoon. He was alone in a net, bowling earnestly at unguarded stumps and teaching himself, he said, to master the leg-cutter. He had, I am sure, the ability, the desire and the application required to be one of the great bowlers of all time, but the physical capacity to establish a claim was denied him.

Trueman, in contrast, enjoyed full blessing of health and freedom from prolonged injury and constructed an astonishingly extensive career for a fast bowler. He played for Yorkshire from 1949 to 1968 and in Test cricket from 1952 to 1965. In his first season, as a youth of eighteen, he had to be carried from the field at Bramall Lane with a strained back and, inevitably, he was occasionally troubled by the temporary consequences of his occupation, but to the end of his playing days he could, if he chose, commit himself to the full vigour of his youthful bowling action. He never suffered the creaking shoulder or the untrustworthy knee as a permanent consideration. 'Look at him,' Bill Bowes once said to me in envious admiration when Trueman, after ten years of fast bowling, squatted on his haunches having completed an over. 'If I had tried that I should never have got up again.'

The particular attitude of rest is characteristic of the coal-mining community from which Trueman derived and presumably heredity did contribute to suppleness and strength, but Trueman's major cricketing fortune lay in his natural bowling action. It was consciously developed and adjusted in detail as advice and experience accumulated but essentially it was a gift from the gods, recognized and admired as soon as seen. Trueman looked a bowler whenever, and whatever, he bowled.

He was unquestionably great not only because he took 307 wickets in Test matches and 1745 wickets for Yorkshire, but because of the impression his bowling created, the imaginations it stirred, the hearts that it warmed. He brought splendour to the cricket of his time.

He also brought controversy through some eccentricities of behaviour, but there was universal agreement that cricket in the 1950s would have been poorer without him. He was always a promise and frequently a presenter of the dramatic. He alerted spectators, as he alerted opposing batsmen. Bumper and yorker and magnetic away-swinger mingled like electric shocks to make both batting and watching a continuous adventure that began with a toss of the head as preliminary to a long, accelerating run-up leading to a wide delivery stride, a beautiful sideways presentation and a flowing follow-through. Culmination was often enough a stare, or glare, of disbelief in the batsman's survival and sometimes an uninhibited comment on the luck of the enemy. Trueman always had breath to spare for an expression of opinion.

From a shortened run Trueman could be a high-grade technician in swing and 'cut' at fast-medium pace and in this manner he determined the course of a Headingley Test against Australia; but in my memory his full glory was epitomized at Lord's in 1956 when he strove through an afternoon to restore hope in a losing battle. He bowled from the Nursery end, at his best pace and with impressive control.

In this attack he created and dominated the atmosphere of play. There was admirable bowling from the other end, but it was background to the battle between Trueman and the Australians. There was no swift batting collapse; Trueman had to wait for wickets and work for wickets and he did not take them all, but the batsmen knew and the spectators knew who carried the banner of England's desperate challenge.

The appropriate acknowledgement was made by Miller. Playing his last Test innings at Lord's he came in when five wickets had fallen for seventy-nine, scored thirty in sturdy defiance and was finally compelled into a catch to the wicket-keeper. Before he turned for the pavilion he looked down the pitch to the triumphant Trueman and waved a gesture of appreciation for the fine outswinger that had conquered him. A great bowling spell could not have been more spontaneously or more generously rewarded and I count the moment among my treasures of cricketing experience.

In the 1950s I came to my own fifties, which is a time of life with sufficient past to induce consideration of the future. With, hopefully, much still to come there is a desire for the preservation of known satisfactions among future changes that must come to a living and developing game. The enthusiasms of youth give little thought to the future; present delights carry a promise of eternity and there is no need for misgiving, because ample time and inexhaustible strength will right any wrongs. Middle age is inclined to more uncertainty, in realization that if things are wrong or may go wrong there is less time left to right them.

Some disturbing trends in the cricket of the 1950s came to the surface to create an urgent problem requiring immediate solution. Wardle challenged customs of behaviour and was rejected by his county and M.C.C. as a touring authority. Illegal bowling actions were condemned and forthright action was taken to eliminate them. These were cricketing aggravations of the day, demanding major surgery but likely to have permanent influence on health only in neglect of that surgery.

Longer lasting in effect were the drifts beneath the surface. Test matches began to overwhelm the first-class programme, with all the competing countries elevated to nominal equality of status and all Test matches expanded to the limits of significance in publicity. The publicity itself sought self-justification through drama and controversy that had to be assumed or created where they were not inherent. One consequence of limelight is comparative obscurity for the rest of the stage and for supporting characters and as Tests and tours proliferated the daily domestic cricket tended to become a background concern for public and players.

In the thinking of the period the ancient distinction between amateur and professional began to appear anachronistic. The move towards abandonment was not regarded as urgent and never became an acutely divisive issue, but proposals indicated the changing outlook that originated the revolution of the 1960s. The case for a common denominator of 'cricketer', with direct payment for all, was advanced on arguments that the amateur would need compensatory payment to fulfil all the obligations being required of him and that the acknowledged professional was suffering unfair competition in the range of perquisites.

The traditionalist could contemplate with equanimity the loss of 'Gentlemen v. Players' fixtures and in theory, at least, reclassification offered wider opportunity for the introduction of part-time players, but there was misgiving that change of status would not affect the amateur only. The professional, I thought, would lose a quality of respect and independence difficult to define but long recognized and appreciated in sport. Professional 'standing' is more than a matter of payment. It is a recognition to be earned and guarded. Professional and amateur alike can contribute talent to a game, but a greater contribution is required from the professional because he has committed himself to the preservation and development of his particular art.

By this definition professional and amateur—whatever the form of payment—undertake different responsibilities and I think cricket, or any other game, will lose a desirable element in a confusion of functions. Events seem to be confirming this belief.

16. New Thinking

A cricketing Rip Van Winkle falling asleep in 1961 and wakening ten years later would have known all the confusion that fell on the character of the Catskills. The decade transformed the face and philosophies of first-class cricket. A trickle of trends that began in the 1950s swelled to floodwaters through the 1960s.

When our borrowed character dozed off the counties were playing twenty-eight or thirty-two matches in the championship. Tuesdays and Fridays were travelling days and Sunday appearances were by personal request and of charitable intent. Summer carried the cricketer through a long-established routine from the net-practice of April to Festival farewells of September. For the chosen few there were variations measured in selection for Test matches or Gentlemen *v.* Players at Lord's.

The touring side fulfilled a programme of thirty-two first-class fixtures, including five Tests, with a closing appearance at the Scarborough Festival, which extended over its traditional nine days and, in this particular season, added the bonus of a match between the Champion County and the runners-up.

With as many as fifty or over sixty innings available to batsmen in regular occupation aggregates of 1000 runs were commonplace. Alley, of Somerset, exceeded 3000 and seventeen others, including one Australian tourist, passed 2000. Seven all-rounders scored 1000 runs and took 100 wickets.

Commercial sponsorship provided cash awards in the Tests and cash and trophies for five individual performances covering the whole season. The advertising potential in cricket promotion and subsidy was scarcely beyond the dawn of realization and exploitation. The boundary fence was uncluttered and the public-address systems concerned themselves with cricket or emergency utterance.

Coming to 1971 consciousness Rip Van Winkle would have found a county championship reduced to twenty-four engagements for all the teams and a further reduction to twenty three-day games under discussion. Two touring teams were in the land, each staying for half the season and playing three Test matches. They came consecutively, overlapping for only a week or two in late June and early July and they did not play each other.

The first-class counties and five minor county teams were involved in a knock-out competition of one-innings, limited-over matches, culminating in a September Final at Lord's and the first-class counties also took part in one-innings competition designed in league form for the Sunday afternoons of the season. A third one-innings competition was in preparation.

As the nominal distinction between amateurs and professionals had been abolished no Gentlemen *v.* Players match appeared in the programme; M.C.C., with two Tests and a Cup Final at Lord's, could have raised no financial complaint and at Scarborough the Festival was confined to a week, containing one three-day match and a single-innings knock-out competition for four invited county teams'

In the first-class statistics three batsmen raised an aggregate of 2000 runs, five bowlers took 100 wickets and there was not one instance of the all-rounder's 'double', as traditionally understood.

Rip Van Winkle would have had to accustom himself to new sights and sounds. Cricket grounds were garnished with eye-catching commercial advertisements and match-endings were followed by the public presentation of cheques for team and individual awards. Commercial names identified the sponsored competitions and television presentation competed with the matches themselves for spectatorial support. The reawakened Rip Van Winkle was in a bewildering new world of cricket. He had slept through a revolution.

Its accomplishment had been more rapid and more fundamental than the most rabid of cricket anarchists or iconoclasts had contemplated. The gates of tradition were found to have surprisingly flimsy locks and hinges.

Cricket acknowledged a need for reform and stimulus by setting up courts for self-examination, but the outcome of their findings and suggestions extended far beyond their expectation and intentions. Their aim was the preservation and prosperity of county cricket in its traditional form of three-day matches and it was essentially to this end that other forms and sponsorship from commercial sources were cultivated.

The original thinking of cricket administration in recommending some one-innings matches was that variety would be introduced into the county season and that a livelier playing attitude would develop, through infection, in the formal championship. Events overtook intentions.

Commercial sponsorship surged through the doorway. Cricket found itself beset by offers of money, with an all-too-obvious possibility that if it were rejected by established authority it might veer towards competing organizations. The Cavaliers of Rothman were countered by the Sunday League of John Player as a children's hour programme of sport on television. To qualify for taxpayer's subsidy a constitutional change to the Cricket Council was accepted. As one-day promotions multiplied the lifeboat launched to save first-class cricket in the counties threatened drowning by its own bow-wave and wash.

The commercial sponsors of sport were not altruistic. They were paying for publicity and it was important to them that their promotions should receive all possible attention. They sought and stimulated television and newspaper publicity and with presentations and prize-money they compensated players for the sacrifice of principles demanded by compressed cricket.

The parties involved, naturally, pursued their own interests, but were not to be blamed on that account. Sponsors advocated one-day cricket as exciting and significant; television was concerned to justify its programmes; players welcomed the enlargement of income; cricket's treasurers were glad of the cash.

In the outburst of promotional activity the ostensible purpose of it all tended to be obscured. First-class cricket was certainly not stimulated by the novelties.

It was made more difficult to present because the programme lost continuity. Provision for the one-day games meant that the season contained days without any cricket for watchers and the reading followers. The habit of attention to cricket tended to be broken. Apprentice players were deprived of a rhythm for their development. Young batsmen in form could not transmit the assurance gained from one innings to another because the lessons learned one day might not have appropriate application during the next week or even fortnight. Weeds of frustration and cynicism grew readily in the stony ground of limited-overs. Who among middle order batsmen advanced to greatness, or had chance to advance, in the 1960s?

One-day cricket, carried to excess as it was, proved not a stimulant for first-class cricket, but a competitor. It took away from the championship all the Sundays and many of the Saturdays. It claimed the names and services of players who would not have been a public attraction without reputations gained in more advanced cricket. It involved players in exhausting, not to say hazardous, road travel at week-ends. It divided interests and ambitions of both players and supporters, though in exceptional cases the possibility of multiplied success did increase public attention.

More subtle influences also contributed towards the denigration of championship cricket. With the game's publicity concentrated elsewhere the championship declined as a talking point and in the prestige of achievement. Yorkshire were county champions five times in the decade of the sixties, yet they were not girded with the glamour of their own teams in the 1920s and 1930s, or of Surrey in the 1950s. They were, indeed, vested with disappointment for not being successful in one-day competitions.

Technical standards of play declined in the championship because lower technical standards were adequate for one-day cricket and incentive was therefore diminished and because three-day cricket became more and more a professional routine, without manifest concern for the interests of spectators. Players and spectators were not inclined to cultivate the difficult arts and appreciation of first-class cricket when the cash rewards lay elsewhere and Test occasions demanded attention for nearly half the season.

All logic implies an inevitable outcome. Without a concentration on first-class cricket there will, eventually, be no home-bred first-class cricketers. Without cricketers of first-class reputation one-day cricket will lose its attraction for spectators and for commercial sponsors. In that event both credit and cash will have disappeared.

My hope is that such an outcome will be avoided by a reversal of current trends, by a rebuilding from the substantial masonry upset in the period of revolution. I do not want cricket of the future to look backwards or to imitate the cricket of decades departed. The qualities of the Golden Age, of the inter-wars era, of the 1950s were appropriate to the circumstances of their time and would be anachronistic in restoration, if restoration were possible.

I want cricket to look forward along a pathway clearly seen and firmly trodden. I want cricketers to be satisfied with nothing less than a full exploitation of their desires and abilities. As I should have deplored the wastefulness of a Hobbs or a Hammond in the chains of a Sunday afternoon knockabout, so I should regret lack of opportunity for future cricketers to find expression of their talents in a game of depth and breadth.

It is my wish for cricket that every age of the past should

contribute to the well-being of the future; that good and harmful should be recognized and retained or discarded. The past has shown what can be done with bat and ball, with material matters of pitch preparation and playing accoutrement and with spiritual matters of adventure, application and enjoyment. The past has also given warning on gambling and corruption, on illegal bowling, on international disagreement and political interference, on unacceptable conduct and on dreary presentation.

I hope the cricketers of today and tomorrow will be able to accept the desirabilities of yesterday not as glories gone but as legacies in transit, capital for reinvestment. Equally I hope the cricketers here and to come will investigate the misjudgements and misconceptions, their own included, and reject the unprofitable because they are trustees.

I feel that first-class cricket—that is cricket at its most advanced development—will not prosper as an appendage of one-day expressions. It must have a life and a will of its own. It must be wanted for its intrinsic rewards. It must see for itself, speak for itself and pay for itself.

Money will not save it because money is not its primary objective. Financial return is no more the driving force of the first-class cricketer than of the surgeon, the painter or the musician. One-day forms are to first class cricket as lighter magazines are to the classics of literature in educated reading—no more than an introduction. When strength and perception increase, the immature reading loses its appeal. Something bigger and wider and more challenging is sought.

So with cricket. When ability and appreciation develop, the simpler forms of the game are outgrown. Yet qualities in unsophisticated cricket and reading remain qualities of appeal at all levels. Childhood readings have a story, an action, as their appeal; so have the immortal plays and novels. Elementary cricket is hitting the ball and defeating the bat and those fundamental desires and attempts are also the life-blood of advanced cricket.

Beyond physical considerations in cricket, the enjoyments of vigour, are attitudes towards the game. These, too, are derived from early experience and are transmitted into higher education. The notions of whole-hearted striving, acceptance of statutory authority, rejection of sharp practice, come from first experience of cricket and are implicit throughout its whole range. Should these basic characteristics be lost, or obscured, during a period of change that period will be unsatisfying, as it was in first-class cricket during the 1960s and early 1970s.

First-class cricket lost favour because it was not played well enough, eagerly enough and with manifest conviction in its purpose. It allowed itself to be swaddled in irrelevancies represented by different forms of cricket, complications of rule and tactics and concern for feather-bedding finance. It became involved in political issues leading to disharmony at international level and it permitted distortion of its own image through breaches of principle requiring public apology.

First-class cricket will, in short, recover esteem when it does itself justice again and when that justice is seen to be done. The soft options of bread and circuses marked the fall of Rome.

17. Purely for Pleasure

Cricket shares with Cleopatra the charm of infinite variety. Attractions in the game range from breath-catching drama to soporific contemplation, from beautiful movement to bounding ferocity, from intense physical effort to a stroll in the outfield or a seat in the sunshine. The pleasures of cricket are wide enough and deep enough to touch all manner of taste and temperament, to serve the cultivated mind or the simple soul, the lifetime or the idle moment.

Cricket's satisfactions are communal and intensely personal. Mine have included:

The feel of flannels

I enjoyed this sybaritic experience from schooldays to the last playing occasion. Discarding the heavier workaday attire for the lightness and freedom of flannels gave a sense of relaxation independent of any prospects of play. I would have tried to play cricket in a hair shirt, corduroy trousers and Wellington boots had need arisen, but the customary costume was, for me, a pleasure in itself. Simply to be in flannels was a contentment of my cricket.

Down the years cricket costume has altered to meet playing needs. The overarm bowler could not maintain his action and his dignity wearing a top-hat and the advances in ground preparation obviated the necessity for brown boots, but twentieth-century cricket has demanded modifications rather than any revolution in basic dress. A cricketer of Edwardian summers would look vaguely old-fashioned on the fields of today, but he would be recognizable as a cricketer.

Fashion changes have been only in detail, whereas tennis-players, for example, have accepted a fundamentally different form of dress. By the trends of today cricket in shorts and even without shirts is conceivable, though presumably climatic and aesthetic considerations will prolong conservatism. The Edwardian might question the logicality of a V-necked sweater against his with the roll-collar for warmth and he would note, as a distinction from his times, the boots now cut away below the ankle and the bulky thigh-padding commonly worn beneath the trousers to counter the bruising inflictions of inslant bowlers.

If first-class cricket should turn further towards the exhibitionism of commercial entertainment identification by numbering might be a future procedure, or the wheel might turn full circle with a distinctive shirt for each player, as the Australian aborigines wore on their tour of 1868. In the ultimate a cricketer could be required to carry a sponsor's name across shirt and sweater and, with a television camera at square leg, there is advertising space on a bending batsman.

Going to the match

Robert Louis Stevenson's assessment of hopeful travel is not always applicable to cricket but going to the match is one of my pleasures. In the days of earliest recollection it was a tram-ride up the long hill to Undercliffe out of the bowl of Bradford's city centre. From tram-stop to ground entrance was only a few hundred yards and there was always ample time in hand, but the excitement of anticipation prohibited walking. I had to run; I might have been missing sight of players in pre-match practice.

Tram-cars could scarcely rate as transport of delight in themselves, but they transported to much cricketing delight in their service during the 1920s and 1930s. 'Specials' ran to Headingley and Park Avenue and Bramall Lane and on a lucky day you might share a seat, or standing room, with a player you were going to watch at play. Herbert Sutcliffe first met Percy Holmes on a tram-car in Leeds—going to Headingley, of course.

Tram journeys stay in my mind as part of a day's cricket at Edgbaston and at the old Aylestone Road ground in Leicester. When two or three of us travelled together we gambled on the ticket-numbers. I have forgotten the rules of our game, which merely determined who paid the fares.

Brighton had the most inviting tram-ride of all, along the sea-front from the Old Ship Hotel to the appropriate stop in Hove. You were going to cricket, you had a sense of holiday and you gave yourself a bonus of ozone on the open top-deck. The most alarming tram-rides to cricket of my experience were in Sydney, where the open-sided 'toastracks' required agility and resolution to embark and a cultivated indifference towards the perils facing a conductor swinging his way along the running-board.

Going to cricket at Lord's and at Scarborough have given me special delights. The approach to Lord's is attractive only in romantic conception because the wall along St John's Wood Road is forbidding and the Main Gate has an institutional appearance, but entry through the Grace Gates never fails to stir my imagination. I always feel as though I am stepping into history.

So it is, of course, and Lord's on a Test-match morning offers the fascination of living history to the observant early-comer. In the forecourt opening from the Grace Gates, in the passageway behind the pavilion, on the grassy mound at the back of the Warner stand there are reunion reminders of yesterday's battles. Casting aside the years and assuming the peak of form you can usually compile a Test team from the conversational groups encountered in a fifty-yard stroll. I know of nowhere else on earth where so much of cricket's flavour is so readily concentrated.

Scarborough at Festival time breathes cricket. Its economy is based on the thousands who choose early September for the family seaside holiday because cricket is being presented at the North Marine Road ground. Hotels adjust themselves to the cricket programme. Shops relate their wares to cricket.

The talk at convivial gatherings, public or private, concerns the play of the day or the morrow. Cricketers are seen on the field and heard, or heard of, in the evenings.

Recent adjustments in the Festival programme and in social holiday habits have cost Scarborough some of its September cricket character. The civic emphasis is not as strong as it used to be. Flags and bunting no longer decorate the main streets and cricket is no longer the dominating theme of shop-window displays. A cricket song or joke is not now inevitable in the variety shows and the Spa is not a recognized place of cricket assembly in the evenings. Scarborough is still essentially a cricket centre during the Festival, but less manifestly so because the motor-car brings and takes away a daily visitation.

The abolition of the amateur cost the Scarborough Festival some of its character. It meant the abandonment of a long-standing fixture, though that might have been necessary anyway and it meant a literal diminution of colour in the occasion. Festivals were less sober-hued than championship engagements. Monochrome of sterner business could be discarded for the brighter trappings of I. Zingari, Free Foresters, Crusader and Authentic in cap and blazer. The generation of J.W.H.T.Douglas could be seen entering the ground already in flannels, sometimes carrying a precautionary umbrella. University colours or an England cap and blazer were not considered ostentatious or out of place, provided they were worn with due qualification and dignity.

Going to the match at Scarborough develops personal ritual as varied as temperaments and time-facility. For some there is sandwich-collecting from a favourite bakery. For others there is the earliest possible arrival to ensure a wanted vantage point, the waiting hours to be passed with book or crossword puzzle. Hendren liked to drive to the ground in an open horse-drawn carriage. My leisurely approach on foot seeks to include a small diversion giving a glimpse of the sea. Down the years from childhood to qualification for old age

Top: P. J. Sharpe in characteristic readiness at slip. The batsman is B. L. D'Oliveira, the wicket-keeper J. Binks. *Below*: C. H. Lloyd, spectacular in the field.

F. S. Trueman entering the delivery stride of a superb bowling action.

G. Boycott, single-minded in batting concern.

Wentworth Woodhouse, one-time South Yorkshire home of the Earls Fitzwilliam, patrons of cricket. *Below*: Bramall Lane, Sheffield, in its last phase as a cricket ground. The viewpoint is from the pavilion enclosure. The stands and the floodlights served football which was played across the far outfield before cricket was abandoned in 1973.

pension I have never gone to Scarborough Festival cricket without the tremor of anticipation that heralds adventure.

Physical responses

Cricket is not the most physically exacting of games, but it does demand strength of arm in specific application, co-ordination of hand and eye, a sense of balance and stamina. A cricketer is not so rigidly bound by the years as, say, a footballer or a track athlete, but he is usually most adept in the prime of life or on the youthful side of it. There are, of course, notable examples of skill and enthusiasm retained to the gateway of old age; W.G.Quaife was still playing county cricket regularly at the age of fifty-six, Wilfred Rhodes was still a Test-match cricketer in his fifty-third year and J.B.Hobbs, 'the Master', made centuries as readily after his fortieth birthday as before. The exceptions emphasize the generality.

Paradoxically, the physical prowess of young manhood is least appreciated when it is possessed. The boy waits impatiently for the peak of his strength; the ageing note with regret the onset of rheumatic twinge and stiffening back. When resources are ample they are not counted. Yet cricket's pleasures do include conscious physical satisfactions. There is a thrilling muscular stimulus in the swift stride and pick-up; in the flexibility of fingers as the ball leaves a bowler's hand; in the vibration that travels up the arms after a full-blooded hit from the middle of the bat. The physical reactions are perhaps more easily understood and more frequently experienced in the negative. Misfielding brings a bruise or a break; imperfect throwing strains a muscle; the ball struck at the bottom of the bat or on the splice may cause a stinging in the hands.

These inadequacies and consequences are known to all who try to play cricket, but the successful accomplishments offer complementary and compensating thrill. The cuddle of the ball safely and comfortably in hand, the impression of elasticity deriving from a flawless drive could, I suppose, have scientific measurement and medical explanation. Cricketers happily accept them as a mysterious but munificent reward from their game.

Sight of the great

My lifetime touches cricket's Golden Age but my time in cricket has left me just outside the boundaries of that glamorous era. Grace and Ranji, Trumper and Noble, Blythe and Bosanquet I know in detail, but only at second-hand by their pictures and performances and by descriptive writing and the folklore of their contemporaries. Their cricketing characters are as real to me as any enchantment, but I have not encountered the actual presence of their greatness.

Within my generation, however, I have known comparable greatness and am duly grateful for the sight and sound and feel of it. Into my span came the mature Hobbs and Woolley and Macartney; the full careers of Bradman, Hammond, Hutton, Compton, of Tate, Bedser, O'Reilly and Verity, of McDonald and Larwood and Trueman and Lindwall; the blossoming of May and of Sobers. Personal observation has given me Hobbs and Sutcliffe in opening partnership, Tyson and Statham bowling together, Chapman, Lock and Lloyd fielding.

Supreme greatness transcends precise definition and analysis. It is an impression. To dissect is to destroy. It needs figures but it cannot be circumscribed by figures; it needs manner but the manner is infinitely variable. It raises an emotional response beyond the bounds of logical argument. It evokes inspiration without envy.

To accord this greatness and therefore to share it vicariously is the highest form of pleasure cricket can give and for me the pleasure is enhanced rather than diminished by a mingling of trust and apprehension. I felt more anxious for Hobbs and Woolley at the beginning of their innings than they presumably felt for themselves. Early dismissal could not lessen them in my esteem but until they were established at the crease I was selfishly fearful lest some accident of cricket should deprive me of the thrill of their splendour, of a basking in their authority.

In county cricket I had to apportion desires and loyalties. When Yorkshire played Surrey I could hope for Surrey all out 125, providing Hobbs or Peter May made 100 of them; Kent or Gloucestershire could be routed for my rejoicing if Woolley and Hammond were left unharmed. This reaction was more than a childish fancy. It remained with me all through my cricket watching, through my years as a professional observer when I was theoretically in lofty detachment. Much the same sentiment apparently affected others. Arthur Mailey has confessed that when he once defeated and dismissed Trumper his satisfaction involved an emotion akin to having 'shot a dove'.

The trepidation experienced when the great began to bat or bowl was vastly outweighed by the sense of wonder and fulfilment when their artistry was presented. On the principle that 'we needs must love the highest when we see it' the great cricketers have contributed to the quality of living. The authority, the mastery, the 'class' that stamps supremacy in any art form initiates a response we can no more avoid than we can explain. Appreciation of the exceptional comes to us as a conclusion reached without conscious steps in logic. Those of us without technical expertise know without knowing why; those with ability and experience of their own recognize without having to analyse in detail. 'There is nothing I can show him,' said George Hirst of the fledgling Hutton; 'You cannot fault his method,' said Warner of the same Hutton a few years later. The sight of Bradman drew spontaneous tribute from the wisest cricketer of all and Wilfred Rhodes was not accustomed to wearing his heart on his sleeve.

A contemporary of mine in school and Barnsley C.C. teams was Harry Bedford, who reached the Yorkshire first eleven in 1928. As a club cricketer Bedford was a useful all-rounder, but Yorkshire's principal interest was in his leg-break bowling and they gave him his chance on an end-of-season tour comprising three or four championship matches in the South. One game was at the Oval where Hobbs made a century. Bedford, who was a delightfully modest and friendly cricketer, told me afterwards that he had been fascinated. 'I forgot everything else when Hobbs was batting,' he said. 'It was simply wonderful.'

This is the beneficent influence of greatness displayed. It expands experience and it elevates us beyond any disagreeable elements in comparison and competition. The quality of true greatness, like that of mercy, is not strained:

> It is twice blessed;
> It blesseth him that gives and him that takes.

Intentions

From its origins and by its design cricket was intended to be a pleasant pastime. The conventional conception of the game pictures good-natured play in a pastoral setting. It has been described as 'the meadow game with the beautiful name' and it has given to the world a message of morality in the phrase 'It isn't cricket'.

The precepts of cricket stand high in the ranking of its pleasures. They remain in the trappings with which it is surrounded and in the sophistication it has developed. Cricket is still supposed to be played, still thought of in generality, as it was originally conceived—in friendly enmity. The pleasantness of cricket has always been its supreme appeal.

Ideals and practices have frequently diverged. There have been ill-tempered cricketers, cheating cricketers, anti-social cricketers. In some periods of its history cricket has known corruption, defiance of law and political encroachment. It has known personal dispute and public discord, but it has not abandoned regret and a sense of shame over manifest shortcomings. Majority opinion wants cricket to be a pleasant game for the gratification of people in pleasant mood.

Players and administrators of first-class cricket have known exceptional difficulties in recent years. They have been required to preserve the essence of their game under pressure from iconoclastic practices. Cricket, like other forms of sport, has been challenged by thinking and behaviour that 'isn't cricket'. In some aspects sport has conceded that foul play may be regarded as fair play. An Association footballer loses no prestige among his fellows and the team supporters by deliberately cheating; he is, indeed, applauded for the 'professional foul' because 'there was nothing else he could do' to save a goal. An athlete is encouraged to belief that the use of medical stimulant is justified by resulting performance. Tantrums on a tennis-court are recognized as tactical ploy or acknowledged with sympathetic applause. A national coach in Rugby Union football has advocated 'better cheating' as the response to successful cheating in the line-out.

Lines at the edges of cricket morality have wavered. Official rebukes to individuals at home and to teams touring have had to be issued and penalties imposed. The fervour of national and local patriotism has occasionally induced crowd-stupidity and the common courtesies have been sacrificed for cash in interviews and ghosted writing.

First-class cricket could, no doubt, be presented and justified as a commercial undertaking, with its values correspondingly adjusted. Its pleasures need not be measured in terms of good-natured striving in opposition, of scorn for the mean advantage, of appreciation without abandon, of contest without controversy. They would have to be different pleasures, appealing to a different breed of player and follower.

They would not be the pleasures recalled and defined by George Hirst when he leaned across the rails of the pavilion balcony at Scarborough on his retirement day and said: 'What can you have better than a green field with the wickets set up and to go out and do your best for your side?'

Cricket is perhaps the most complicated of all games in subtleties of technique and tactics, of actions and reactions, of variety in self-expression. It meets the challenge of physical endeavour, mental alertness and reflective satisfaction, but it has a simple heart. It provides every reward in recreation, but the full rewards are available only from pleasant cricket—cricket without rancour, cricket without selfishness, cricket with purpose essentially in itself.

Cricket can be played in this way from the school field and the village green to the Test match arena. It can be played in this way by the casual participant and the dedicated careerist, amateur or professional. It can be played in this way as a pastime or as an occupation. It can be seen and enjoyed in this way by those without playing talent or experience.

High-level cricket might give way to a public presentation involving bats and balls and stumps, with significance in politics, in commerce and in sociology. It might become a means to an end beyond and more exacting than itself and in such destiny there is no right or wrong but thinking makes it so. All I claim for my own belief and for those who have formulated and reflected that belief is the certainty that cricket without a pleasant character would be cricket transformed and diminished.

18. Yorkshire

Yorkshire is the Lone Star State of cricket and Yorkshiremen, like Texans, are all invested with a composite character universally recognized at a level of caricature. It is a character partly self-created, partly imposed and now established by both anticipation and cultivation.

Yorkshire cricket is accorded by the cricketing world in general a quality of its own. The reputation, being of practical benefit, is welcomed by Yorkshiremen who have come to emphasize and guard it, even to an extent of accepting some of the less desirable by-products. Yorkshire cricket is supposed to be played the 'hard way', with competitive success a primary concern. It is seen as the cricket of championships and leagues, of determined batting and painstaking bowling; as cricket of serious mien and an unsympathetic, not to say contemptuous, view of failure and misfortune. Summary is traditionally expressed in the observation 'We don't play cricket for fun', variously attributed to Wilfred Rhodes and Leonard Hutton.

This soft impeachment is acceptable to Yorkshiremen on an agreeable definition of 'fun'. Yorkshiremen do not find their cricketing fun in a purposeless pastime, in idle occupation with hit or miss experiment involving no consequence. They do find 'fun' in the struggles of cricket, the endeavour towards successful batting and bowling techniques, the outwitting of opponents, the satisfaction of ability displayed and potential realized. The worst failing a Yorkshire cricketer can show, to Yorkshiremen, is the slap-happy, thoughtless attitude. The fun of the game comes from solving its problems, from treating it with respect as a worthwhile undertaking and, of course, from winning.

By repute Yorkshire cricket lays too much emphasis on winning. The Yorkshire retort would be 'Are both sides not trying to win then? Was the contest not arranged on an intention to determine who would win?' There is right and wrong in both arguments. No team, no individual, can lay too much emphasis on winning as a desirable and fundamental objective, provided endeavour remains within the legal and moral framework of play. Teams and individuals would be uncomplimentary to opponents, to spectators and to self-responsibility were they competitors without trying to win. The Olympics claim that it is more important to take part than to win needs extension; the greater importance is to take part in an endeavour to win by acceptable means.

In the Yorkshire philosophy of sport it is impossible to be too keen on winning a competitive engagement. The desire to win is a virtue unalloyed, but some practices arising from the virtue can tarnish it. Cheating is an obvious example. Manipulation of the rules and customs to an opponent's disadvantage is another. Instigation and cultivation of a disagreeable atmosphere comes within a grey area of tactical behaviour.

Most of us, I suspect, have stepped into the grey area at some time or other in our sporting behaviour; have sought an advantage by unwarrantable appeal, by wasting time, by a practice honed if not sharp. In the ultimate assessment I presume we shall all seek mercy rather than justice.

The Yorkshire reputation for playing 'hard' cricket is not acceptable to Yorkshiremen as an accusation of approving the grey area. W.G.Grace was not a Yorkshireman, but he had his little ways. D.R.Jardine was not a Yorkshireman, nor was 'bodyline' bowling a Yorkshire conception. It was not a Yorkshire bowler who shouldered a running batsman to the ground in a Lord's Test match. Yorkshire cricket has received public rebuke for misconduct on the field and in the dressing-room, but Yorkshire cricket authority has invariably acknowledged error and sought correction.

The Yorkshire hardness, attributed and cultivated, is a defensive quality expressed in the form of aggressiveness. It is resistance to challenge, unwillingness to bend the knee or doff the cap. It is the cricketing representation of independence. Reflection extends beyond cricket to the mill where the owner anticipates being addressed as 'Fred' and where the traveller is given an egalitarian 'luv' with request for the fare. The spirit of independence is, of course, two-sided. 'Fred' is expected to know faulty workmanship when he sees it and to say so in forthright manner. Weak or vacillating management wins no approval.

Yorkshire's hardness in cricket stems from self-criticism. The weakest periods of county performance have been those in which players were most easily satisfied with themselves, the strongest those in which the ultimate possibilities of achievement were seen and sought. The directive and cohesive influence exerted by Lord Hawke forged strength into a team that became more than its sum of individual talent. The leadership of professional expertise established by Rhodes and Emmott Robinson brought business-like efficiency. Sellers and his players constructed a close community of ideals and interests. The successes of the 1960s sprang from shrewd observation and cricket thinking by Close and Illingworth.

In its development stage and at its peaks of achievement this Yorkshire hardness was admired throughout the cricket world. It lost favour when it blemished the character by being an end in itself. Lord Hawke was seen as putting Yorkshire interests and his own above all other. Efficiency in the 1920s was seen as grim-visaged and short-tempered in any frustration. The self-discipline of the Sellers era avoided criticism perhaps because it had not become oppressive when cricket was interrupted. Close fell from favour because he defended his purposes against unacceptable means of attainment.

That Yorkshire cricket should create a character for itself, or have one imposed, presupposes attention being paid.

Yorkshire cricket has commanded attention from inside and outside the county because the natives have shown an uncommon aptitude for the game. Yorkshire is not recognized as a cradle of cricket in the sense attributed to the Kentish Weald and Broadhalfpenny Down, but there was Yorkshire cricket of sufficient significance to justify newspaper record in the 1770s and teams were raised in the name of Yorkshire before the formal institution of the county club.

Any claim to a Yorkshire 'gift' for cricket is tenable only on the same terms as Welshmen are granted a gift, or flair, for Rugby football. There is nothing in Yorkshire air or Yorkshire turf that makes a cricketer. Yorkshiremen have no superiority of eyesight or muscle; they are neither freaks of nature nor descendants from Olympus. Their tradition of cricketing dexterity is probably derived more from the by-products of economic development than from any other single factor. Sheep and steel and coal and cloth were basic ingredients of Yorkshire cricketing skills emerging from the Industrial Revolution.

Cricket of the Dales, the Wolds and the Plain of York showed no particular quality or character when Yorkshire was essentially a county of agriculture and domestic industry, but concentration of mill and mine and warehouse in the West Riding seems to have had significant influence. Rapid growth of population in a small area produced more players and keener competition in play. Sport in various forms was a natural reaction to the exacting labour of daily life; without the safety-valve of cricket, football, pigeon-fancying and whippet-racing—to say nothing of darts and dominoes in the ale-house—the economic grind might well have proved unendurable and anarchic.

In the course of generations mine and mill created strengths and dexterities that were applicable to sport. The saying that 'If you want a fast bowler shout down a pit shaft' had a basis in reality. Cloth-making and engineering gave both a delicacy of touch and a development of the left hand.

Years and lifetimes of piece-work inculcated a spirit of determination and endurance. The qualities required for winning a livelihood revealed themselves in sporting approach and activity.

The proposition of left-hand facility deriving from factory practice carries logic but of course it cannot be accepted without reservations. There were left-handed cricketers before the factory age and there are left-handers outside industrial communities. The high proportion of left-handers to be found in Yorkshire and Lancashire cricket could be no more than a reflection of numbers. Where cricket is played by the many, more left-handers would naturally be expected than where cricket is played by the few. Similarly, from a dense population a larger supply of skilled players is likely to emerge. By this reckoning there should be a sufficiency of good cricketers in Yorkshire simply because Yorkshire has a population of millions.

Manpower resources alone would not necessarily create a cricketing community. Additionally there must be a cricketing interest and a cricketing opportunity. The Yorkshire interest presumably devolved from the widening national interest during cricket's nineteenth-century development and opportunity came because improvised implements were readily obtainable and people were available for a game during breaks in working hours. Cricket was a convenient and rewarding pastime.

It was rewarding not only through intrinsic pleasures but as a means to social distinction. The good cricketers were local 'somebodies' and the best cricketers could use cricket to escape from mine and mill. Although the industrial south and west Yorkshire spread far the communities within the general area were small and closely knit. Centres of interest tended to be in a specific pit or foundry or workshop, inducing a sort of family loyalty and a competitive urge between unit and unit, as between brother and brother.

The playing representative was invested with responsibility

made all the more evident by a close contact in work and play. If you dropped a vital catch or failed with the bat at a critical moment you were likely to be reminded of your shortcomings through the next week's working hours. Equally manifest, however rough the expression, was prestige accorded to success.

From this foundation grew personal resolve to improvement and collective desire for competitive success, grew the hard fibre in play, the league organization. Casual cricket was to be deprecated because it did not meet life's philosophy.

Again, the development can be advanced only as a broad consideration. Yorkshire cricket extended beyond the industrial areas; some cricket in Yorkshire was inconsequential; not all Yorkshiremen were prepared to work hard at their recreation and not all determined cricketers have been Yorkshiremen.

The composite character attributed to Yorkshire cricket derived from geographical as well as human factors. Yorkshire is a northern county and the soft, turning pitch is a commonplace—or was before the days of compulsory covering. Spin bowling was rewarded, if spin bowling were accurate; defensive batting skills had to be learned if long innings were to be played. In such conditions bowlers and batsmen taught themselves to wait, to persevere and to concentrate. The decisive point of a match could occur in an hour, in an over, and the successful side or individual was the one ready to grasp and hold the fleeting opportunity.

That is the essence of the hardness characterizing Yorkshire cricket in its minor and major presentation. At its best it is illustrated in determination to redeem apparently lost causes, to face difficulties with unflinching resolution, to acknowledge defeat only when the last ball has been bowled. At its worst it becomes an attitude of arrogance, a blinkered view and an irritable reaction. In the one form of expression Yorkshire cricket has won the respect and admiration of the cricketing world; in the other it has incurred dislike.

All the great Yorkshire cricket has displayed the common element in its heritage, but individual exploitation has been as widely different as the personal characters involved. The same theme has produced infinite variations. Far back in history George Anderson's Yorkshire independence was recognized in his reputation as a trusty batsman in time of trouble and as a man of principle in his forthright stand against apparent injustice. 'Happy Jack' Ulyett was a Yorkshireman in hitting fifty adventurous runs against Australia after his captain had bidden him take care. 'I rather felt like hitting them, my lord,' was his subsequent self-justification.

George Hirst crystallized the Yorkshire hardness in his declaration 'It's thee or me for it', as he took bat or ball in hand. His friendly smile neither obscured nor diminished the challenge. Wilfred Rhodes was always uncompromisingly an opponent, even in net practice. Roy Kilner could murmur 'I'll never learn' when he was caught in slips or covers after waving a speculative bat, but he turned pale and sick in nervous exhaustion after particularly exacting bowling occasions. Herbert Sutcliffe's authority lay in the self-confidence that permitted no consideration of failure. 'I love a dog-fight,' he confessed. Australian bowlers appreciated the Yorkshire characteristic in Maurice Leyland, that most placid and contented of cricketers who determined with rare precision the difference between a Test match and a Festival.

Hutton illustrated the Yorkshire hardness in his ceaseless self-examination. 'It's nice batting, when you've made 100,' was his concession to himself. Trueman's flamboyance and garrulity disappeared when he brought concentration and his magnificent skills together in his hours of glory. Wardle and Close and Boycott gave offence only because they presented the 'unacceptable faces' of their native zeal.

Yorkshire cricketers have come in all shapes and sizes. They have been grim and gay, dashing and dour, calm and excitable, strong and weak. Their batting has ranged from the speculations of David Denton to the immobilities of Louis

Hall. An Oldroyd and a Leyland could bring their contrasting methods into the same team and both be counted typical and unmistakably Yorkshire. The imperturbability of a Sutcliffe was carved from the same millstone grit as the passion of a Macaulay.

There is no end to the individuality of Yorkshiremen playing cricket. They reflect themselves in all their variety of skills, moods and temperament, but together they have a common end, born of circumstances and accumulated tradition, that is their hallmark. The belief that England cricket is strong when Yorkshire cricket is strong does not imply that England teams need seven or eight Yorkshire players but that there are Yorkshire players good enough as individuals to be chosen for England and who will bring to the national team a valuable quality of approach that is characteristic of Yorkshire cricket.

Yorkshire cricket supporters are reputedly myopic and parochial—with a reservation that they are prepared to disadvantage each other. One Yorkshireman of passionate county loyalty once observed to another, in praise of Yorkshire rather than in deprecation of a great 'foreigner': 'Hobbs couldn't make runs against Yorkshire.' Provocatively, the second conversationalist, who had been brought up on *Wisden*, murmured: 'I wish I had £1 for every century Hobbs took from Yorkshire bowling.'

'You can have more than that,' came the sharp retort. 'I'll give you £10 for every Hobbs century if you give me £1 for every time he played against Yorkshire without making a century.'

The offer was accepted, though on an understanding that no money would change hands because the acceptor knew he could not lose. Education through argument was reward enough.

Corresponding licence to correct is assumed by Yorkshire supporters in their relation to Yorkshire play. They are harsh taskmasters. Let Yorkshire fall from the grace of expected supremacy and internal complaint is registered in manner ranging from annual meeting protest to a slow shake of the head and a bewildered 'Nay, it won't do.'

'It won't do' for Yorkshire supporters, of whom more than 10,000 are county club members, when Yorkshire cricket is not manifestly a powerful force in the land. Promise unfulfilled 'won't do'; a diet of hope continually deferred causes flatulence. Intolerance and protest are immediate reactions to the cardinal sin of ineffective cricket. Players in a weak Yorkshire side have found more comfort in away matches than in appearance on home grounds. Comment of complaint remains in years of glory, but there is forgiveness in it; the dropped catch, the batsman's mistiming, are condemned as a failure, but explained as an accident. The strong Yorkshires could afford occasional misfortune.

The weak Yorkshires are viewed with a sense of frustration and deprivation, like an ailing business. Workers are not working and management is not managing properly. 'Nay, it won't do,' applies to a whole concern as much as to an individual.

Yorkshire spectators have, or had, the reputation of being more knowledgeable than most in cricket, but the impression probably derives more from environmental influence than from any possession of native wisdom. The truth may be that if Yorkshire crowds did not concentrate on the cricket there would be little else of attraction on their home grounds. Tea and social gossip in the marquee or on the lawns are not features of cricket in Bradford and Leeds. Nobody basked through an idle hour in the shade of a tree at the late and lamented Bramall Lane. It is true that the bars are open all day, but Lord's not Leeds has a famous Tavern; it is true that wool is bought and sold at Park Avenue as well as on the Bradford Exchange; it is true that knitting needles have played *obbligato* to centuries by Hutton and Boycott; but by enormous majority Yorkshire cricket attendances are for the delights and rigours of the cricket itself and by watching and listening and assuming and believing an education is absorbed.

I doubt if Yorkshire crowds can rightly claim any superiority in appreciation of cricket's more advanced technology and tactics. As many naïve and ill-informed observations on play and players are to be heard in Yorkshire as in other places, but I think the comment, wise or foolish, tends to be more heartfelt. Yorkshire cricket has a strong sense of family association. Playing successes and failures are taken home to influence the domestic atmosphere. A cricket topic is virtual guarantee of appearance among 'Letters to the Editor' in Yorkshire newspapers. Yorkshire shortcomings or dissensions are regarded by Yorkshiremen as a concern for internal consumption only and outside comment tends to provoke a closing of ranks on a principle of 'my county, right or wrong'.

By this interpretation Wardle could be condemned for disturbing Yorkshire cricket but raise sympathy on his omission from an M.C.C. tour; Close could be acknowledged in error as a Yorkshire captain but still supported as an England leader and Trueman's bumpers for Yorkshire could be given an approval not accorded all bumpers—especially those delivered against Yorkshire. Young players are granted a credit of goodwill on the assumption that without some merit they would not be playing at all. Early inadequacies may be tolerated, but debit entries are soon made against the account. Promise must turn to performance measurable in runs or wickets.

After inspection proving satisfactory the Yorkshire player becomes an accepted member of the cricket family. He receives a treatment of domestic familiarity, which implies a consistent welcome, the muted congratulation that takes success for granted and unquestioning support in time of trouble. The final attribution is to the greatest of individuals and teams; they are given the respect and authority that transcends investigation or analysis. George Hirst going in to bat, Wilfred Rhodes and Hedley Verity going on to bowl, Holmes and Sutcliffe opening an innings, the outstanding teams taking the field received tribute warmed by vicarious pride. They were beyond compare and beyond criticism. They were county possessions, like the Dales and York Minster.

In days before handclap in unison and monotonous chant became the fashionable and moronic comment Yorkshire crowds could fairly claim to have been both a feature of cricket and a force in cricket. For visiting sides they served as a fourth dimension of challenge, additional to the batting, bowling and fielding. They were another opposition of will, another encirclement.

A young batsman bowled first ball felt the finality of a High Court sentence in the roar of acclaim at his dismissal. An Australian has confessed that he needed all his Test match nerve to await the umpire's decision, which was 'not out', when Bramall Lane with one voice appealed for l.b.w. The spectators were playing in the match. The harshest criticism a Yorkshire crowd can make is not impolite comment, not adjuration to improve; it is indifference. When Yorkshire crowds cease to care Yorkshire cricket must take deep concern for its health.

For their own players Yorkshire supporters maintain a general routine of appraisal. They are inclined to look before they leap.

Recent trends in cricket will, I feel and fear, modify some of the Yorkshire peculiarities. Attitudes and customs are changing with changing cricket organization and presentation. The Yorkshire belief that if you cannot win there is virtue in striving not to lose must weaken under match conditions that insist on victory or defeat, however artificially ensured. Television has introduced a common denominator into crowd behaviour, suggesting that pitch invasion by small boys and simple-minded seniors can be a practice in Bradford and Bombay alike. Professional techniques and ambitions tend to promote a universal sophistication that diminishes distinctions between Yorkshire cricket and Somerset cricket and Australian cricket and West Indian cricket. Covered pitches and limited overs will—as they are presumably intended to do—eliminate the particular skills and opportunities of locality.

In that outcome there would be no advantage or disadvantage in being born and reared to Yorkshire cricket. In that outcome cricket in general may or may not benefit. It will certainly be different.

Index